Olivofonics

Other books that have been written by Francis A Olivo. I also plan on writing more books during my life so please lookout for them. Francis A. Olivo is a member of the "APPA" American Philosophical Practitioners Association. All the books that I write are meant to be fun and educational.

Olivononics (Oh-Lee-Vo-Non-Ecks): A Philosophy in Self-Rehabilitation. This book is great for anybody wanting to get released from prison earlier than normal. This book looks at the philosophical question of is it possible to earn an early release from prison. The book is written in easy to understand English and designed for people coming to philosophy for the first time.

Olivononics Two: How to Think Like a Philosopher. This book is great for anybody thinking of taking philosophy in college and would like to get a small taste of what philosophy is all about. This book would also be great for people who have trouble with critical thinking or if a person has trouble figuring out what they want.

Fancy Frank's Bartender's Guide. This book goes into detail about liquor, brandy, cognac, and other mixed drinks. It has a page on common slang and terms used by bartenders. It's easy to read and lots of fun. This book also makes a great gift.

Olivofonics

Small Business Management & Philosophy for Beginners

Francis A. Olivo

Writers Club Press
San Jose New York Lincoln Shanghai

Olivofonics
Small Business Management & Philosophy for Beginners

Writers Club Press
an imprint of iUniverse.com, Inc.

For information address:
iUniverse.com, Inc.
5220 S 16th, Ste. 200
Lincoln, NE 68512
www.iuniverse.com

The Author is not responsible for your
Business failures.

ISBN: 0-595-17472-8

Printed in the United States of America

Dedication

I'm dedicating this book to Miss. Margaret Berkley. Ms. Margaret Berkley has shown me the importance of patience and virtue. I've written many letters to her and corresponded many different idea on business and philosophy. The world needs more individuals like Ms. Margaret Berkley in it. Thanks for always being there to talk to me and give me hope and encouragement. One day we will walk hand and hand on the beaches of California and make many fond memories together.

Epigraph

Careful planning is more than common sense. Common sense is more than careful planning. The world is truly a complicated place. I know this because I'm a small business entrepreneur and philosopher. Things we believe to be true we consider to-be our knowledge. Things we don't consider to be true, we have no knowledge of. Until there is a universal knowledge we can only believe in what we believe to be true. The world is truly a complicated place full of many different beliefs that people believe to be true. So knowledge is power but only if you believe it to be true. Francis A Olivo (1963-?)

Open-mindedness is the key to understanding our complicated world. Many individuals speak of being open-minded, basically because it sounds really cool and is socially acceptable. However, unfortunately, open-mindedness is somewhat beyond the grasp of the adverage individual. In order to be understood, we must first seek to understand. It's possible for two different dictionaries to have two different definitions of the exact same word; therefore it's also possible for two different individuals to have two different meanings of the exact same philosophy.

My understanding of open-mindedness is to be willing to consider all premises and or propositions. It doesn't matter if you agree to them or not. In order to be considered open-mind, you must simply be willing to consider anything, whether you agree with it or not is beside the point. If, however, you're unwilling to consider a premises or a proposition, you cannot consider yourself as being open-minded. There is a myth that says, "If you don't agree with a premise or proposition, then you're not open-minded." This is not true in any way shape or form.

You can still be open-minded, even if you say no to the premise or proposition. Like I said earlier, in order to be open-minded you simply have to be willing to consider any premise or proposition. I'm personally about 99% open-minded, there are certain things that I'm not willing to consider and therefore, unfortunately, I cannot claim to be 100% open-minded. Nevertheless, at least I understand what it is to be open-minded and so do you.

Contents

Foreword

There are certain truths that are true no matter how much we may deny them. In the economic realm, for example, you cannot legislate the poor into independence by legislating the wealthy out of it, nor can multiply wealth by dividing it. The government cannot give to people what it doesn't first take away from other people. And that which one man receives without working for, another man must work for without receiving. This was what a man called, "Kenneth W. Sollitt" wrote and I have quoted.

Lots of philosophers have talked about the human mind. There're so many written things about the human mind I couldn't quote them all. Today for the second time I'm going to talk about my opinions of the human mind, which I think is one of the most fascinating things in the world. This is the second time publicly that I'm going to share my personal philosophies about the human mind.

I've written two philosophy books that are currently released now. Olivononics A Philosophy about self-rehabilitation and Olivononics Two How to think like a philosopher. In both books I talk about the human mind. My philosophy on the human mind has never been heard until I wrote those two books.

Most people believe that the mind has two parts, the conscious and subconscious mind. We feel guilty about something when there's an unbalance in our minds between the conscious and subconscious mind. Yet nobody ever thinks of where the conscious or subconscious mind comes from.

I believe the egg is the subconscious mind and the sperm is the conscious mind because the sperm cell moves on its own toward the egg but the egg has no control over moving. Our subconscious mind can't control our body movements but does exist and lets us know about rules and ethics. The egg can't move so therefore it must be our subconscious mind. The egg has a mind because it's alive and waiting for the sperm cell. The sperm cell becomes our conscious mind because we know when we are moving it's our conscious mind that makes our decisions to move. The sperm cell swims toward the egg, who can't move under it's own power, so the sperm cell is showing instincts. Instincts are non-taught biological capabilities. The sperm cell shows this instinct by swimming toward the egg. Once in the egg the minds do not splice together, which forms both a subconscious, which is the egg's mind, and a conscious mind, which is the sperm cell's mind. In the case of twins the egg splits into two even pieces. Both twins have a subconscious and conscious mind, which means that a mind can be split but cannot splice together. If the mind can split apart than it's possible that the mind was split off of your parents mind who's was split off of their parents mind and so on and so on until we get to the first mind that came into existence. If the mind isn't split off from some original mind from thousands of years ago, how do we explain instincts? When a baby is born at the hospital the doctor doesn't give the baby crying lessons. When a baby horse is born the mother horse doesn't give the colt standing lessons, yet the colt's instincts tell it to stand right away. What are instincts? Where do they come from? A mother doesn't teach her children to lie to get out of trouble yet children instinctively know to lie to get out of trouble. We may never know or understand where the conscious and subconscious mind comes from, or we may never fully understand instincts. I can't explain where or how the first mind came into existence.

Nevertheless, the problem exists that man, as Aristotle said, "All men have the need to know or understand the world around them." Now I ask you what do you think of my philosophy about the subconscious and conscious mind? Is there any way possible that my philosophy could in fact be true? Things we believe to be true, we consider to be our knowledge. Things we don't believe to be true, we have very little knowledge of. So knowledge is power but only if you believe it to be true. Francis A Olivo.

Acknowledgements

Before graduating from high school, Miss Stephanie Starkman started working as a waitress in a local restaurant in a small town. After demonstrating her abilities in dealing with extremely difficult customers she was promoted to assistant manager at age 19.

Miss Starkman later moved to the Twin Cities Minnesota and took a position as a cashier in a convenience store plus also worked part time as a waitress in a restaurant. The management knew that Miss Starkman worked hard and could deal with any type of situation due to her understanding of the philosophies of ethics. A local business owner told Miss Starkman about a job opening in a bank.

After a short interview Miss Starkman was hired as a teller. In as little as four years Miss Starkman was promoted to vault teller. Miss Starkman also worked part-time at a liquor store putting her total hours worked per week up to 70-hours. The liquor store acknowledged that Miss Starkman was an extremely hard worker and would go out of her way to please the customers. Miss Starkman was asked to become the store's manager at that point in time.

After taking the management position she moved up to full benefits and received a raise in salary every single year. Miss Starkman's name was getting around as a truly gifted and hard worker. A liquor enterprise, consisting of 8 stores, approached Miss Starkman and offered her a larger salary to manage one of their liquor stores. In the two years that she's currently worked at her new job she's received two additional raises and excellent benefits as well as owner and other business owner's recognition.

Miss Stephanie Starkman hasn't filled out a resume in nearly ten years because of word of mouth of her experiences. Every liquor business owner speaks of Miss Starkman with the Utmost highest respect. Miss Starkman made all these achievements due to her impeccable working reputation. Miss Stephanie Starkman never forgets that customers and coworkers always come first. Miss Starkman is always the first to pat an employee on the back and tell them great job. With her understanding of the philosophies of reality, nobody can pull the wool over her eyes. Miss Starkman is a prime example that hard work and intelligence is the key to becoming a small business manager. Miss Starkman doesn't know what her future holds; however with her initiative, we can safely count on it being a bright one. Without initiative there can be no future in small business management. I've personally interviewed Miss Starkman on several different occasions and she's a wiz at small business management and her philosophical views are inspirational. It was a true pleasure to meet this extraordinary woman.

Miss Kassandra Canning but prefers to be called simply K.C. Is going full time to the "Le Cordon Bleu Culinary School" in Minnesota and still made assistant manager for a liquor store due to her hard work and dedication. K.C. will graduate in April of 2001 and probably take a managing job in her field. Dedication and hard work always pays off. I wouldn't be surprise if she started her own business. Currently K.C. is only limited by her youth, however, I believe she's bound for greatness in business.

Spencer A. Rogozinski took an old building for little money down and started his own business called, "All Star Cards" which he made a living off of for three long years while going to computer college full time. If Mr. Rogozinski can accomplish this while going full time to college, imagine what he can do after graduating? The future also looks bright for Mr. Rogozinski.

All these people have what it takes to be small business managers. The key to his or her success was hard work and dedication. Never under estimate the under dog, they're the ones that pull the hardest when it comes to striving for excellences. If you ever get a chance to hire these special individuals I personal suggest that you do so. These people are on their way up in the world.

Introduction

Most of us remember reading about the midnight ride of Paul Revere. Yet few realized that Paul's other fame came from his small business. Paul was a silversmith who often rode from town to town to sell his handmade silver and copperware. An original Paul Revere bowl today would cost an estimated $9,000. Real prosperity escaped Paul during his lifetime, but it can be reality for the businessperson of today.

The memory of flavored seltzers that his family served at home and a guess that people of today wanted lighter, less calorie, but still delicious, soft drinks prompted Alan Miller to found the "Original New York Seltzer Company". When Miller started out in 1982, he had to mortgage his house and secure a loan from his family to meet the $70,000 start up costs. Today, the worldwide sales figures for Original New York Seltzer amount to over 150 million a year.

Ben Franklin was the first self-made millionaire, in America do to his small businesses. Yet few people know of Franklin's entrepreneurs. Almost everybody at that time had his or her own business. Very few people worked for other people in those days.

Not everyone who owns a business will get famous and rich. However, a successful small business owner, also called an entrepreneur, will earn a very respectable living if he or she makes sure that the business has all the right planning. What is the right planning? Well, first, you need to make sure that you're cut out for entrepreneurship. It's not for the weak hearted. Are you willing to work hard, take chances, and assume responsibility and authority? Can you give orders and handle difficult people? If so, read on. This book will tell you in detail what it takes to be a successful entrepreneur and go into your own small business.

There's an audience out there that wants and needs the products and service that you plan to offer. Make no mistake about it. You, of course, have what it takes and enough experience to give that audience what it wants. But you need a plan. A good business plan begins with your purpose and then explores your personal and financial needs, plus location, inventory, equipment, and employment needs. Without a sound plan, you run the risk of continual surprises and eventually even failure. Starting your own business doesn't have to be a gamble. With the information in this book, you'll be able to put together a plan that will guide you through the intricacies of starting your own business successfully. Success is getting what you want. Happiness, is wanting what you get.

The only thing small about a small business is it's actual size. The majority of new jobs created in the last decade came from small businesses, and more than 99% of the businesses in America are in fact classified as small businesses. So when you begin your own small business, you're in a big business.

The Small Business Administration "SBA" defines a small business as any which employs fewer than 500 employees. In actuality, more than half of the companies in this classification have from one to four employees, and almost 95% of all small businesses have fewer than 50 employees. If the business that you're planning is in this small category, then you qualify for a number of incentive programs, and you fall under the jurisdiction of several agencies, which can offer you help. Not to mention free advice on the subject of starting your new business.

Small business is an officially identified interest group tracked by the "SBA", the "IRS", the Department of Commerce, and numerous other state agencies. Because of the special needs of small business, these agencies have initiated a number of incentive programs for you. The small business innovation research grant, small business set-asides for United States government procurements, health insurance, tax write-offs for business owners, and tax-sheltered retirement plans for self-employed.

In addition, if you're a woman or a member of a minority group, the government offers even more assistance. Female-owned businesses get preference when competing for government procurement projects. And if a large business is awarded a contract, the government often requires that subcontracting work be given, when ever possible, to female-owned businesses. The same provisions apply to minority owned businesses. Although, the government specifically for minority owned businesses sets no contracts aside, all contracts that have small business set-aside provisions give priority to minority owners.

Chapter One

Business Planning

Strength is needed in each of the four important areas when you're entering the entrepreneurial world: yourself, the money involved, potential customers, and your family. Out of the four "yourself" is the most important key to success.

You must be a kind of person who's willing to work long hours with optimism. The first month and in some cases years of a new business can be hard, because you'll have no good idea of how much money you'll end up with after all your hard work. You shouldn't be going into business just to make a quick million and then get out. You should be starting out because you have an idea that has a market, and an expertise that will help you deliver on that idea.

If you already have experience in a business similar to the one you plan to begin, then you have a good start. If you're planning to work with a partner who has that experience, and you can provide the business know how, that will also help.

One of the many mistakes that new entrepreneurs often make is to decide to go into business without having any clear idea of exactly what type of business they would enjoy. The counselors at one local Small Business Development Center or "SBDC" tell tales of women who think they might like to start a florist shop because it sounds like a pleasant type of business, or to start a personal shopping service because they themselves enjoy shopping. In the first instance, the counselor will quickly perceive that the client has no real experience in the floral business. Carrying heavy potted plants is not particularly pleasant, and the rough hands that come from flower preparation are even less pleasant. The personal shopper has some idea of the foot soreness that can come from trying to locate the perfect gift, but she has yet to discover whether she has the expertise to shop for others and locate gifts pleasing to a new, unknown customer. The counselor speculates, that both of these clients are not yet ready to put down money to start a new business. What do you think?

Expertise and experience are two important elements in the successful business formula. You need to know your business inside and out; otherwise, you'll be a novice to entrepreneurship and to your product or service as well. Make no mistake about it; you must have a business plan. Not only will the lack of knowledge complicate your life, but it will also become quickly apparent to your customers. So, if you haven't got the expertise for the business you dream of opening, either get it fast or hire somebody who can supply it, or change your dream to one to which you can contribute real know how. Not to mention we're talking money here. You're not going to get a shot of your own business without spending a few bucks.

Running your own business means you'll have employees working for you. Are you sure that you can give orders, supervise people, make out work schedules, and establish a fair and equitable way of dealing with those employees? Can you establish a good relationship with them, without getting so friendly and casual that you lose their respect? Can you be firm if they try to take advantage of you? At the same time, can you be understanding and lenient with them when the situation demands? If you've had previous experience, either as a manager in somebody else's business or as a foreman or supervisor, then you already know your qualifications in this area. If you have no such experience, then you will have to live and learn. This book will help you in many ways but it's only a guideline to get you started.

If you've taken business courses in school, you already have some idea of record keeping, inventory management, and the personal requirements that you face. Or maybe you haven't had any school background, but have acquired your experience on the job, working for somebody else. That experience will be a big bonus for you now.

If you have no business background, then you need one of two things: a partner who does have this background or a trustworthy employee with business experience. Not only do you need to trust that employee's discretion and honesty, as he or she handles your business records, but you also need to be sure in the knowledge that he or she will be in your employ long enough to get the business well established. If you have the needed business background, or can hire people with the character, background, and experience required for your business, then you can look at the next factor, which will affect your decision to go into business, which is money.

Before we talk money may I recommend a way to judge people? People often ask, "Do you have ethics?" Ethics comes from the Greek word "Ethos" which means character, which is confused with morals, which is a Latin word meaning customs. Once again morals is confused with yet another word "Etiquette" which is a Greek word meaning coming up to the required social standards or well disciplined or basically accepted norms of a polite society. So, do you want somebody with character? A criminal has character. Do you want somebody who has customs? Gangs have customs. Maybe somebody who understands etiquette is the answer? If you must judge somebody may I recommend "Virtue"? Virtue is the long out look of what a person or company has done in relation to ethics, morals, and etiquette. The big picture so to speak. If you look at how a person or company has done in the long run you're looking at that company or person's virtue. I'll talk more about this subject in my book, "Olivononics Two" (Oh-Lee-Vo-Non-Ecks) How to Think Like a Philosopher. ISBN#-1583480595098266. Now let's talk money.

Starting your own business will be somewhat easier if you have some money saved. Also, your potential investors will feel more secure if they know that you are willing to risk your own savings in your new business. And it helps if you have saved enough to show potential investors that you can handle finances and aren't given to foolish spending of money.

The amount of money you need to save depends on the number of factors. First you must work out a business plan to determine exactly what it will cost to get your business started. Once you know your start up costs and have some idea of how much you'll need in order to remain in business long enough to get your name established, you can figure out how much you need to finance. I'll go into more detail latter in this chapter. Often, you can get some credit from the people who will be your suppliers. Do you know how much credit they're willing to give you? If so, you can figure that amount into your beginning finance. Example, I bought a used car lot for $35,000. I had no cars to sell. A car auction vendor gave me a $25,000 line of credit "holding my car lot for collateral" to bid on their cars at the auction and I would make monthly payments on them. My goal was to sell the cars for $40,000 and pay off the loan quickly.

Other than that idea you'll more than likely have to borrow the rest. Do you know where you can get financing? Have you talked to bankers or potential investors, friends, family, and associates? You don't need to get real financial commitments at this stage in your plan. However, you should make sure that there is a good potential for financing you new business.

If it looks as if you have that potential, then take a look at the salary and profit you anticipate getting out of your first year of business. Will you be able to live on it? Will there be enough not only to support your personal life but also to help the business grow? If so, then keep on going. If not, don't despair. There is always the possibility of making your new business a partnership. The old saying two heads are better than one.

There're two types of business partners who help with a start up business. The first type is a partner that has the experience and expertise you lack. The second and my favorite is the business partner, which

FRANCIS A. OLIVO   5

supplies you with enough financing to get the business up and running. That's only if you have trouble securing financing on your own. No need having a partner if you don't need one. Don't get a partner just because you have cold feet. There is also legal ramification, of having a partner.

Before even considering the legal ramifications of taking on a partner, ask yourself if the person you're contemplating sharing your new business with is somebody you can trust and get along with. Is he or she somebody you can work well with?

Choosing to take on a partner limits how you can legally structure your business. Although two or more people may organize as a partnership or corporation, only businesses with single owners may operate as a sole proprietor. Operating as a sole proprietor sounds attractive because it gives you a lot of independence. On the other hand, taking on a partner can give you a big boost, both in handling finances and responsibilities. In the decision making stage, you should be aware that your choice can make a difference between a no go and a viable new business.

Another vital factor influencing the success of your new business is the available market for your product. Perhaps the first question to ask yourself is whether there's a demand for the product or service you plan to offer. If the answer's yes, then you have a bit of research to do.

First of all, take a look at other small businesses in your community. Whether, they are like yours or not, see if they seem to be doing well. If the economic climate in your community is favorable to small business in general, then it will probably be favorable to yours. Don't stop there. Look in your area at businesses that are similar to the one you plan to start. Are they doing well? Is this type of business doing well through out the country? The answers to these questions will help you to predict the degree of success that your business is likely to achieve. However, that's not written in stone.

Finally, observe the people with whom you plan to do business. Can you describe them? What they want, hope, needs? Do you know their current shopping habits? Are you planning to offer them something new and different, possibly even better than what they can already buy? When I owned the car lot, people would come in and ask, "How much down and how much a month?" They didn't even ask how much the car was to begin with. Will your new business offer enough of an incentive to make them change their current shopping habits in order to do business with you? People are sometimes unwilling to change because changing can be stressful. If you believe that your business has what it takes or better yet you have what it takes take the big plunge.

If however, after answering these questions, your idea seems weak, take another look. Thinking about your idea in the light of what you've learned about the potential market, or reconsidering your planned location, may enable you to go ahead with a business about which you're very knowledgeable. However, the definition of insanity is doing the same thing over and over again and expecting a different result. Think clearly on this or be domed to the insanity of wishful thinking.

If you've answered the preceding questions, you now have a pretty good idea of whether starting a business is a good idea for you. However, what about your family? Are they ready to stand behind you, to pull in their belts if the first few months are a little lean financially? Do they understand what you want to do, why you want to do it, and what will be involved for them? Do you have their encouragement and support?

If your main reason for going into business is to make money, have you thought about whether you could make more by changing jobs? If you don't have your family's support for your new business, finding a higher paying job may be the answer. You maybe interested into going into business because you want independence and a chance to try your wings. If you are and you can balance the emotional, financial, and personal involvement demands of the business and your family, then you may be ready to move ahead with your plans, However, make sure that your family gets and gives the emotional and financial support, and the personal involvement that you and they will need. That in my opinion should go without saying.

Developing a business will require more of your time and energy than working for somebody else. Such high demands need high commitments from both you and your family. Every time that I've started a business my friends and family got more excited and involved in it than me. They start off slow and then really get into it. Without family support, you may feel all alone in your undertaking. During the trail periods of new businesses, family support alone can help overcome the hardships that you might face. Not to mention you'll find out who are your real friends. Hardships can be very stressful and both your family and your business life can be affected.

There are ways to reduce business related stress and friction in the family. First, you should openly discuss business attitudes with your family. Explain how the business decision will affect them, why you're considering a certain business, and ask them for their support. Ask them for specific non-financial assistance for a time when you think you'll need it. Almost all people liked to be needed and thanked. Remember, however, the business is yours. You shouldn't expect others to have the same attitude and commitment to it as you have. This is your dream, not theirs.

Your family will be more understanding if you involve them in the planning process. Explain the good and bad points of the business you're planning. If the business will not have many customers during the start up period or during the off-season, explain this to your family. Making them aware of what is taking place can relieve stress of slow times. It can also bring innovative ideas from supportive relatives. One husband and wife who are in business together explained the ups and downs of the business to their children. Their 10-year-old daughter wanted to help mom and dad in the off-season. The little girl put things that were in the back room or otherwise hidden in other areas of the store. She found a way of displaying and marketing slow moving inventory. After her displays attracted the attention of the customers, sales of these items increased. As a reward, her parents gave her more responsibility and let her share in some of the profits. The daughter didn't bring great wealth to the store but she did increase sales of slow moving items and learned a little about small business. When you provide family members with the knowledge necessary to run a business, you create a small army of highly trusted supporters. Everybody makes out on the deal.

Financial support can come from a number of sources: banks, partnership investments, and government subsidized loans. However, for many small businesses, family is the source. Before asking family members for financial assistance, you should prepare a business plan for them, and ask them to review it. You should give them the same information you would give to a banker. Don't presume that your family should loan you anything. If you ask for a financial commitment, let the future investor make an educated decision based on the information. Even if the investor is a family member.

If relatives offer to lend you money for your new business, ask them how they would like the money paid back. Work out such problems before the loan is made. If possible, have an attorney draft a written agreement, or do it your self. Then sign the agreement and ask the person making the loan to sign it as well. Whoever lends you money will be more interested and supportive of your business if you tell when you can repay the loan. The owner who doesn't commit to repayment schedule early in the business often creates a situation in which family members end up not talking to each other. Relationships with family, especially financial relationships should have all the respect of any other professional financial dealings.

As the owner of a business, you must have control at all times. The rules for family employees should be the same as those for all other employees. This is true even if the family member is an investor in the business. Before bringing a family member into the business, evaluate the skills of each potential family employee. A father may be an excellent mechanic, but be a terrible salesman. If he is used as a salesman, he may lose business for you. Even if your father doesn't take a salary, it would be difficult for you to fire him. From the beginning, a business must be treated as such. Notify family members immediately if they are not meeting your standards. Sometimes, it's more valuable for you to hire and pay outside employees who are experienced and expected to obey the business rules. Do not allow family members to weaken your management authority. It's hard to ask your husband not to help or your wife not to help. It's even harder to pay bills with no money.

There are many good reasons to go into business for your self. Although skeptics are always telling us that the failure rate for new business is almost 90%. The U.S. Small Business Administration's 1990's report on small business and competition states that, "Small businesses continue to make important contributions to the economy, generating innovations, employment, and income in both good times and bad. America is now entering the "Age of the entrepreneur." The entrepreneur has been creating new directions in the present economy. This shouldn't be surprising.

Over the last decade, through good and bad economic times, the United States has seen the addition of 60,000 to 90,000 new businesses each and every year. In 1986 alone, small business created over one million new jobs, while large business created only 100,000. This growth has been nationally recognized as the key to the United States recovery from the economic recession of the 1980's. However, money is not the only thing that motivates people to open their own business. Often the need for self-fulfillment or a desire for independence is the really influential factor.

The U.S. Army had a theme, "Be all you can be". The success behind that campaign was the desire for self-fulfillment. The person who is motivated to go into business is also the person who wants to maximize his or her potential to see what they can achieve independently.

In small business, success is relative. Some entrepreneurs are obvious financial successes. Many others reach different levels of success. Success for you, maybe earning extra money to do the things that you wanted to do. It may mean being in business until you obtain the type of job you want outside of you business, or maybe to get money together, to send your children to college? The truth of the matter is that success is only based on your opinion of what success is. Things you believe to be true, you consider to be your knowledge. Things you don't believe to be true, you have no knowledge of.

Psychologists and Social psychologists have rated individuals accomplishment as a highest human value. Once individuals have taken care of their basic needs like shelter, security, food, and family. The individual has a need for self-actualization, or realizing their fullest potential. Business success is one of those methods where an individual can attain this feeling of self-fulfillment. Entrepreneurs are individuals who have a high need to succeed. I know because I'm one of them. I'm a writer, and I have enough rejection letters to fill a pickup truck. Yet I now have three books published and one poem. I'm successful. I never give up on anything. Independence is great.

Too many business owners don't begin any concrete planning until they determined their business location. Then they get out the graph paper and blueprints to map out the office floor plan, showroom, and locations of outlets and equipment. Since your business requires an investment of thousands of dollars and thousands of hours of your time, much of which goes for other things besides location, doesn't it make sense to give the same attention to your business plan? A good business plan will function much like a blueprint, in that it will clearly show you where you are going, what you will need, and how much it is likely to mean to you in actual dollars and cents.

A good business plan begins with several elements: clear description of the business, its location, its structure, and its market, as well as notes about the competition. Before you spend a penny, you should also have a clear idea about your employment needs, management personal, their necessary qualifications, and the need and qualifications for any employee, which means you too by the way. Even more important is a concrete financial plan, which will detail your start up costs, inventory, operating costs, your prospective earnings, and information about any loans you will need and your method of repaying the loans.

Sounds overwhelming? Getting caught behind the eight ball is overwhelming. This section of the book will take you through the steps of creating a business plan with a future. Nothing is overwhelming if you simply take it step by step. I'll review the plan like this, and then you'll be able to use it to go carefully through the conception and creation of your own business. Not only will your plan provide you with a thorough management decision-making guide, but it will also provide bankers and investors with financial document that will demonstrate the earning capacity of your business.

The first step in creating a good business plan is to have a clear purpose for the plan. Your main purpose, in the beginning, is usually to obtain financing. Your secondary purpose is to create a structure that you can use in getting the business located, staffed, and operating.

Begin with a description of the new business as you envision it to be. Is it a new business, or are you taking over an existing business? If you are beginning an entirely new enterprise, what is its purpose? Where do you intend to do business, maybe on a small local level, or statewide, or internationally? With wholesalers, retail customers, or a specifically defined group of trades people? If you're taking over an existing business, you will need to describe it, its good points, and any problems that you may need to overcome. What is the stated purpose of the business? Your plan should tell any investor exactly why you plan to open this business. Is there a perceived need in the community? Briefly describe this need and the way in which you plan to fill this need.

The location section of your plan must describe exactly where your business will be located and why, also why you feel that location will be the best. As any realtor will tell you, the three greatest factors in determining the investment value of a property are location, location, and location. I remember hearing this in high school. Your location will determine not only the value of the actual property on which the business is sited on, but also the success or failure of your business. If you're located in an out of the way hard to get to location, then you'll have some difficulty getting customers. Unless you're selling life giving kidney machines people are unwilling to go through the effort to find your business. If you are located in a highly visible area, but don't have very much parking, people may go to the competition to have some place safe to park their cars. I own a new pickup truck. Somebody flings his or her car door into my truck in the parking lot putting every little ting in my truck there. I look for safe places to park my truck to prevent that from happening again. If your business only caters to a small geographical area, and people will not travel out of their way to get to your business, you better plan on being located very close to the people you plan on doing business with or offer something that they must buy or need.

Generally, there is three major factors that will help you determine the viability of your location: your target market, your type of business, and your location or area of trade. The people in your target market are important to your business plan. First, you must know where they're located. Are you catering to a wealth segment of the population? Then you should make sure that you're convenient to those neighborhoods, or to the areas where they already shop. Is your stated business purpose to take advantage of an influx of people to newly developed areas of town? Then locate near those areas.

Study the buying and shopping habits of the people you want to reach. Are they mall shoppers or people who prefer small individual businesses? This factor can be crucial in determining the success of a retail store. Although service such as realtors and hairdressers don't depend on visibility of location to attract their customers, customers expect them to be easy to get to. Wholesalers don't need locations with high visibility, but they do need good location to save on gas for deliveries.

The type of business you're in will also determine the location that will work best for you. Many retail stores carry highly specialized merchandise that's not readily available to the customer. These businesses don't rely on visibility to attract customers, but instead the limit of availability of the goods will attract the customers to come and buy what they want. For businesses like this high traffic locations are not crucial and the new business owner can save money for buying a place that's not in the high market areas. For businesses that carry goods that are widely available, it's crucial to have your location in a high traffic area to get sales. Convenience is the key to marketing goods that are widely available. These guidelines for retailers may also apply to the service business as well.

If yours is a business for which the customer comes to you, then the need for high traffic location increases as the need for and the availability of the service increase. At tax time, a taxpayer will drive a considerable distance to talk to an accountant about preparing their income tax forms because time is limited, availability of trust worth accountants is limited, and it's a specialized service. However, if it comes to donuts people will buy at the most convenient place they come to on their way to work. For the wholesaler, the best location is the one best to reduce gas prices. Access to major highways and easy accessibility to major shopping areas are far more desirable than high visibility.

The third major factor in determining your location is your area of marketing. The distance determines the area of marketing that your average customer will travel to do business with you. Some businesses, such as gas stations and corner stores, have very little or small marketing areas, sometimes only a few blocks. People simply don't go out of their way to do business with this type of business, because they offer only convenient goods and services, which don't need any comparison-shopping. If your business falls into this category, then the number of similar services or stores in that area determines the viability of your location. How many convenient stores or services can this area support?

Other businesses have a fairly large area of trade, because they carry more competitive goods and services. People perceive differences in price, selection, and quality of goods and services, and so will travel several miles in order to do business with the place they perceive most likely to fill their needs. If your business falls into this category, then you have more latitude in choosing your site, as long as it's somewhat central to the population you're trying to market to. Perceiving is the reality that people live in. If you can perceive your goods and services as high quality people will come and buy. I talk more about reality in my book "Olivononics Two How to Think Like a Philosopher". Yet still other businesses have huge areas of marketing. People will travel hundreds of miles for a certain goods, antiques, fine art, and specialized services. In this case, your location is best determined by your own requirements, deliveries, site needs, and parking.

Finally, for businesses, the area of marketing is determined by the ability of the business to get to the customer. Electricians, tow trucks, or any other professionals who go out to the customer must choose their business location to be central to the population. Only you can determine how far you're willing to travel to perform your services, and so your area of marketing is determined by this and by the location of your target market.

How do you determine a location central to your target market and yet situated in an area that can support both you and your competitors? Here's where a bit of research will help. Your SBA and the local SBDC can supply you with a lot of data about the population. Or you can study the census data at your local library. Statistical Abstracts of the United States, published by the Census Bureau, is available in most libraries; the entire census report can usually be found only in those libraries, which are government document repositories. These abstracts can give you a wealth of information about the area in which you want to look at transportation, growth, average wages, educational, and recreational facilities. Your research should include primarily four things: the population, the number of businesses in the area that are similar to yours, average number of people per stores, and growth per year of the area. To get the answer to average number of people per store, divide the population by the number of similar businesses. Then figure out how many customers you need to support your business. If "Statistical Abstracts" don't break down the population specifically enough (as in very large cities), then your own municipal bureau of records should be able to break it down. If, you can clearly see from the information that there's enough population to support both you and your competitors, you may have found a good location. However, remember when dealing with municipals they're the one doing you the favor, talk to them respectfully.

The next step in the plan is to decide or define the way in which your business will be structured. You have three basic options: Sole proprietorship, partnership, or corporation. Sole proprietorship is simply a business owned by and operated by one person or family. This person or family is solely responsible for all business debts and who receives all the income and rewards from the business. And yes you can consider a family as having sole proprietorship of a business. Sole means one, however, sole proprietorship can also mean one family.

In a partnership, two or more people operate and co-own the business. If you plan to organize a partnership, you must have a very specific agreement defining the rights and obligations of each partner. You and your partners will share both income and losses according to the terms of this agreement; your agreement must also specify what is to happen in the event of the bankruptcy, retirement, or death of any partner. With this arrangement, you no longer bear sole responsibility for your business debts. A partnership is an excellent way to acquire some of your financing; it's also a good way to gain an expert in the areas where you lack specific knowledge about your business and its operation. However, don't take on a partner just because he or she has money to get you started. It'll only hurt you in the long run.

The final way to structure your business is as a corporation. If you choose this option, you must file legal papers and pay fees to the state. As a corporation, you can sell stock in your company. You can also offer benefits such as health, life, and accident insurance to your employees; deductions for such benefits are not available to sole proprietorships or partnerships. And, as a corporation, members of your family can invest in and hold stock in your business without becoming actual partners with all of the obligations of partnership.

Once you've described your purpose, location, and structure, your business plan should address the way in which you intend to market your business. This part of your plan involves describing the ways in which you intend to make your business appealing to your target market and the ways in which you plan to communicate that appeal to your audience. Be as specific as possible.

If you don't feel that marketing is your strong point, get outside help. Your local SBDC can provide free expert counseling on marketing techniques. Or consult a local college or university. Often professors are willing to advise you or to assign your business to their classes as a special project. But don't skimp on the marketing portion of your plan. Even the best conceived, and financed business can fail if it neglects to address itself to the available market.

If there're other businesses like yours in the market, you'll have to get your customers by luring them away from those competitors. But first, you must determine exactly who or what your competition is. Even if there're no similar businesses in the area, don't assume that you have no competition. In determining your competition, you must ask yourself the question, "Where do people shop now to get the same stuff that I'm selling?" You need to be aware of all the alternatives of the other businesses.

The big financial plan, the go or no go of the planning process. More than likely you will at some time need to seek financing for your business. The best time to seek financing is before you need it. The best place to seek financing depends on a lot of factors; there are, however, numerous sources for financing a new business. The first and most common are through a bank. Banks tend to be conservative when it comes to funding new businesses, but if you have a venture, which interests them and appears to be profitable, then they may be prepared to make a loan. Have your business plan with you when applying for a bank loan they're going to read it.

You can also attempt equity financing. This involves sharing the profits with other investors it may even involve sharing some of the control of your business. But when times are hard, equity financing through the investments of friends, relatives, employees, or brokers may be a viable way to begin your business.

If you plan to operate either as sole proprietorship or partnership and if you have no intentions of incorporating, then you maybe able to apply for equity capital through the SBA under the Small Business Investment Act of 1958. Under this act, the state law to provide funds for entrepreneurial businesses charters small business investment companies. These companies will usually take greater risks than a regular bank; however, in return for their investment, they may require some say in the way your business is run.

The SBA can in fact lead you to other ways to finance your new business. SBA loans are in fact hard to get and usually come in a form of a guaranteed loan, and will be issued only if you can prove that you have no other way of getting financing on your own. SBA loans are hard to get, but certainly worth a try.

If you have a poor credit rating, save time and start getting it straighten out as soon as possible. Work on your credit as you save up money to open your new business. I've seen business plans take a year to put together, mostly hung up on the financing part of the plan. The SBA in your area, give free counseling to people wanting to learn more about financing a new small business. Free advice can sometimes be the best advice.

Chapter Two

The Legal System

There are many good attorneys practicing law. They've usually had at least four years of college plus passed the bar exam in their state. The bar exam is the states way of limiting the available work to only those who are very proficient in the legal system. If a person claims to be a lawyer but didn't pass the bar exam, it's safe to assume that your wasting your money on a con-artist. Only deal with lawyers who've taken and passed the bar exam in the state in which your opening your business in. No matter how much money a person can save you by being a make believe lawyer, it'll be worthless in the end. Always ask if the lawyer your planning on using passed the bar exam in your state. If the lawyer passed the bar exam in a different state they may not be allowed to practice in your state. Never forget this, it'll save you money.

The fact that most lawyers are smart doesn't necessarily mean that they're all useful to the small business owner. You must find an attorney you feel good about and can understand clearly. You're going to need that lawyer for small jobs and for major emergencies. There will be business moves you'll want to make, such as remodeling your store or enlarging your parking lot, which are sometimes difficult to accomplish without legal assistance. Because an attorney is an important part of your business, you should include legal costs as part of your projected expenses, just as you would the costs of raw materials and supplies.

Do you understand why a small business owner needs to line up an attorney before anything even happened yet? Do you know what to look for in an attorney? You'll need an attorney for unexpected emergencies. You might receive a summons with your name as well as your business name written behind the word "Defendant". This little gem is called a lawsuit. This is what I mean by emergency. This is not the time to go digging in the yellow pages looking for an attorney. You need a lawyer who knows and practices business law. You don't want to pay a lawyer $90.00 per hour to learn while your paying the bill. There are lawyers who practice nothing but business law. Almost every lawyer has a favorite part of law that they wish to practice.

The small business lawyer is the most valuable in easing your way through the never-ending rules of owning your own business. Your small business lawyer is specifically trained to guide you through the maze of government regulations. Some of these regulations are written and some are unwritten. You may not realize it, but you are assumed to know all of these rules. If the government writes the rule down or if a court records the results of a lawsuit, you are held responsible for knowing all about it. Anything for a laugh I guess.

Written laws, called statutes, may require the help of a lawyer to understand. One really big example is the "Uniform Commercial Code" that governs contracts between merchants. The code is a simple set of rules for resolving disputes. It deals with questions like, "When is an offer really accepted?" "What happens when you leave something out of a contract?" and "Who wins when two contracts disagree?"

The Commercial Code also has all the rules that govern the relationship between you and your bank. Although it's easier to read than other things in the law, the problem with using it your self is finding a specific answer among the thousands of pages. Attorneys, on the other hand, generally know the rules by heart. Even if they don't know the rules you need, they can locate it very quickly.

Written laws are gathered into codes. Each governmental agency has its own codes. The various branches of the federal government have codes, the IRS "Internal Revenue Service", for example, have a code and so do your municipality. The federal code is bound in many volumes and is usually kept in the town's law library, if the town has one. A small town's code may be kept on the court clerk's desk in a loose-leaf notebook. A small businessperson can become confused and overwhelmed by the sheer volume of government codes and regulations.

Codes contain both the law and directions on how to go about getting what you want from the law. Getting what you want is called, "Procedure". When you're talking to your lawyer about getting a new sign for your store, you're really asking about what procedures are needed to get your sign okayed. Sometimes the procedure is easy and involves only filling out a form, having somebody there to let an inspector in, and paying a fee. At other times the procedure involves scheduling a hearing before a zoning body, notifying all possible interested people, and making your most persuasive presentation in an open meeting. Whatever the procedure, your lawyer can quickly locate the law on your topic and advise you as to which procedure will do what you want to be done, and if need be to tell you that it can't be done.

Unwritten law is known as common law. Procedures involving unwritten law almost always require a lawyer, because this law isn't available to you in a code. Common law comes from court decisions handed down over a period of years. Court decisions involves common law are gathered into casebooks, which include reports of decided trials. Believe this or not, the businessperson is held responsible to know which set of facts has previously won in the courtroom. When you make a business decision, you've supposed to make it in light of what you know. Since you're presumably informed about these past decisions, the court system finds it fair to judge your contract by these legally established rules. That's the big theory, and that's why you need an attorney for a dispute involving the common law.

Common sense doesn't translate into common law. You can in fact have lots of common sense and still have no understanding of common law. You need an attorney to deal with common law or common law will deal with you. Never forget this simple advise.

A retainer is money you pay a lawyer to represent you, usually for a particular service or event. Be prepared to retain your lawyer if you have work you want done right away. Pay by check and get a receipt because it's also a tax write-off. The retainer is not the entire fee that your lawyer might charge you it merely binds a lawyer to an agreement between you and the lawyer. The retainer does go toward the final bill that the lawyer will give you at the end of whatever your having them get done for you. The fees is determined by the lawyer as to how much time and resources he or she has tied up in representing you. The fee or bill is usually due the day of completion. However, some lawyer may or may not agree to payments. The lawyer is a businessperson too and if you think the fees are to high you might be able to talk the lawyer into lowering their fees until you get on your feet. Lawyer are individual businesspeople just like you, and they run their business anyway they see fit. Some lawyers set their fees and won't budge. Others may provide the same service and will work for a lot less in the hopes that your business will grow and pay full rates later on. If you don't ask, you don't get.

If you ever have a dispute with your lawyer, call your state bar association. Explain your problem and ask what you should do. Follow the advice you receive to the Tee. In a really outrageous situation, you may have to sue your lawyer for malpractice. Even the best lawyer occasionally makes a mistake. If your lawyer has made a mistake such as not filing something in time, and your business suffers because of that, your lawyer or lawyer's insurance company should pay or some how make it right. Anything short of outrageous conduct on the part of your lawyer is difficult to prove.

Some lawyers offer what's called a small business package, which is like a legal insurance policy. The lawyer will, for a set price, counsel you on the form of business you should use, create and register the business, and obtain all customary permits and licenses. There are advantages to such packages. First the lawyer already knows what to file and how much time it'll take so that speeds everything up, it's convenient for you, and it usually costs less than hiring a lawyer to do it from scratch. You should ask exactly what's covered in the business package. However, some lawyers may use the small business package to lure a new small businessperson into the office in order to sell other legal fees or services at much higher prices. What you save taking the package you lose in other legal fees. So a small business package is only as good as the lawyer who's offering it. It's your money and unless you've got a lot of it, make every penny count.

Most people who own a small business do so as a sole proprietor, probably because it's the least complicated way to do business. There are few requirements beyond a city or county business license. If you do business under a name other than your own, you may be required to register as doing business under a fictitious name. You may also be required to publish notice that you're using the fictitious name. In a sole proprietorship, you take all the risks but you also take all the profits. You are the business and you own everything used in the business. All debts are your debts; all income is your income. Any income tax comes out of your pocket. If you or one of your employees is injured in the course of your business, the injured person can sue you for damages. If the injured person wins in court, you could lose everything the business owns plus everything you own as well.

As a sole proprietor, you must buy insurance against this liability. However, this can only insure against reasonable foreseeable disasters, and not every possible situation can be fully covered. Let's say that one of the companies that make you parts goes out of business. Because you can't find another company to make the part for you, you also go out of business. Some times the sheer size of the disaster can cost over your insurance coverage. When you operate as sole proprietor you assume all responsibilities for your company and employees.

Incorporating your business, only if done correctly, limits your liabilities to whatever you have invested in the business. Incorporating your business also creates a shield between your private holdings and your business holdings and or creditors. Sometimes, however, these creditors demand your personal property before they'll extend any credit for your new business. Only those creditors who agree to look just to the business for payment will be barred from looking at or taking your personal property to collect payment. Unlike the sole proprietorship, a corporation isn't part of you. It's a whole new entity. It's much like a person with whom you have a close relationship. Incorporation grants the business owner protection from business creditors. The state limits abuse of this advantage by setting up strict formal requirements for the creation and operation of a corporation.

Some states require a minimum number of stockholders in a corporation. If you have more than one stockholder, you should contact your lawyer and direct him or her to draft a stockholder's agreement reflecting how you and the stockholders have agreed to run the business. Yes, you heard right, agreed to run the business. Stockholders can and often do vote to protect their investment. I've seen pictures of people who've founded a business hang in the main lobby saying, "Our founder so and so". The reason this person is the founder and now the owner or president is because this person was simply voted out of the presidency by the stockholders. This person is no longer the president or owner but only the person who started or founded the business. So by doing incorporation on your business you maybe voted out because the stockholders feel somebody else is more capably of running the business.

There are two basic types of corporations, and the government taxes the ownership of each differently. The "C" corporation, which is the standard and most common corporation, is taxed first on what the corporation itself earned. Then the owners of the shares pay personal income taxes on the money they received as dividends from their investment in the corporation. In effect then, the money is taxed twice. Until recently, corporations were taxed at substantially lower rates than most successful individuals. After tax reform, double taxation almost always means more total tax payment.

The second form, and my favorite, corporation is called, "Subchapter S or S Corporation", essentially passes profits and or losses through the corporation. Income is attributed to the owners in direct relationship to how many shares they own. Owners are charged with the income, whether or not they actually receive the money. After tax reform, the "S" corporation became a highly desirable entity for tax purposes in some states. Yet in other states, the "S" corporation isn't available: it's taxed the same as the "C" corporation. States like California doesn't recognize the "S" corporation as far as for tax purposes. In order to establish an "S" corporation, all the stockholders must elect that option, which means each one must sign the election on federal from number 2553. Almost any business lawyer can help you on filling out this form.

If you don't like the idea of a corporation, double taxation, and other excessive paperwork you may consider having a partnership. It's important to create partnerships in a way that's suitable for everybody. Forming partnerships can be dangerous if not done correctly. If your going to be partners with somebody and be responsible for that partners debts, contracts, and decisions it's a good idea to state the terms of your partnership before anything is signed. Example; you take a partner who has lots of experience but little money, that person maybe entitled to a share of your business and make you sell the business to get half the money.

General partnerships are those in which both partners work in the business, have equal rights to manage the business, and can make promises or incur debts for the business. The Uniform Partnership Act, which has been accepted in most states, establishes rules for general partnerships.

General partnerships don't need a written document, nor does it need to be registered unless it's doing business in a fictitious name. A partnership resembles a sole proprietorship in that each partner is liable for the decisions and contracts made by any other partner in the partnership. This is true even though a partner agrees to something the other partner appears to have determined not to do. If a partner appears to have authority from the partnership to sign an agreement, he or she can bind the partnership: the partnership will be held accountable for the terms in the contract that only one partner has signed. This is called, "Apparent authority" and is binding in the eyes of the law.

Partners usually share equally in the profits and debts of a business. When a partner transfers ownership interest in the partnership, the new owner receives the right to profits. A purchaser doesn't receive the right to participate in the business management unless all the remaining partners agree to it. This is because partners are held to very high standards in both their dealings with one another and other people that the business deals with. These standards are called, "Fiduciary Duties", the highest duty of loyalty by law. Fiduciary duties require partnerships to promote the interest of the partnership above their own, and to truthfully inform one another about the opportunities available to their business. This way partners can't grab opportunities for themselves or other businesses they might own if that opportunity would otherwise go to the partnership. Theoretically this fiduciary duty is above price. As Plato wrote, "We all have the idea of perfect justice in our minds, however, to project the perfect justice is impossible in an imperfect world."

In a general partnership, each partner has an equal right to manage and conduct the partnership business. Partners are personally liable for all partnership obligations. Unlike a sole proprietorship, the partnership isn't liable for each partner's person debts. The partnership ends with the death of one of the partners. It also dissolves if a partner becomes bankrupt or legally insane. And "No" you don't lose anything if your partner is going through a divorce. Your partner might have to sell their share of the business but you lose nothing.

If you ever have any questions about rules or laws about business, always talk to your lawyer. Never assume anything about the laws of business. People have and will do again make assumptions about laws and rules about business or they might plainly ignore a law or rule of business and invest money in an unlawful business. These people normally lose big time. Check the laws of your state, county, and city before investing in a new business. The money you save can be spent on more important things for your business other than making things right again after finding out that you've got to make some changes to get legal. A lawyer can save you money in starting a new business. Make sure when you make a business plan it includes lawyer fees. Lawyer fees are also a tax write off so save the receipts.

Chapter Three

Business Insurance

On July 7, 2000 at around midnight to two in the morning a storm poured about 10 inches of rain in about two hours on my town of Eagan Minnesota. The rain quickly made a flash flood that caused flood damage to homeowners and small businesses. One man of 20 years old was killed in the flood while he was trying to swim in a drainage ditch. He was sucked into a water pipe that was full of water and died of drowning. This all happened in the town I was living in yet I was not hit at all by the flash flood. People lost cars, homes, and one man lost his life. The mayor called this storm, "The 500 year storm." Our drainage system was only able to handle the so-called 100-year storms. Many people were unable to get any money from their homeowner's insurance because they simply didn't have flood insurance. This flash flood was unforeseeable.

Insurance is a technique for transferring a risk from one party to another. There are two basic types of risk, speculative risks and pure risks. A speculative risk is one that can lead only to a loss or to no loss. Speculative risks are things like gambling and investing. When opening a small business your taking a speculative risk that your business will be successful and you'll make money. You also take the risk of the business being a failure and you lose all of your investment. In other words it will make money or lose money. When you buy a building or a truck for your new business those things are then subjected to what's called pure risk. The building could be hit in a flash flood or burn to the ground. The truck could be stolen or wrecked. So that's a loss or no lose situation, which is a good description of pure risk. Going into business is a planned risk or speculative risk. Wrecking a truck isn't a planned risk or well it better not be planned because that's insurance fraud. Insurance is concerned only with pure risks, not speculative risks. And, for insurance purposes, risk can be defined as the chance of a loss.

There are methods available to help eliminate the chance of loss to his building and truck. First is avoidance, you can eliminate the risk of losing the building by not buying it in the first place. Retention means to retain the risk of lose by assuming all the consequences of any misfortunes that may befall the building. It's not a good idea to assume all the responsibility. Transfer the risk to another party, which in most cases would be an insurance company. This transfer of risk is called insurance.

An insurance company gathers statistical information from it's past experience with thousands of other small businesses. From this information it develops probabilities of loss for each type of business classification. Based on these probabilities, an insurance company determines the premium to be charged for insurance. A premium is charged to each insured individual or business. The insurance company then pays all claims to its insured out of these accumulated funds. A firm purchasing insurance pays a fixed premium, thereby transferring to the insurance company the risk of a potentially larger loss. In return, the insurance company promises to pay in the event of a covered loss.

For example, let's say that the insurance company of the homeowners has determined that in their particular county only, chances of flash floods are one in every 500 years. So this flash flood will only happen every 500 years. If the total damage is one million dollars every 500 years and the insurance company has 1,000 insured. The insurance company has to charge a minimum of $2.00 per year per insured homeowner.

1,000,000 divided by 1,000 = 1,000 divided by 500 years = $2.00. If they charge $100.00 per year they make a profit of 50 million dollars with a payout of one million. The $100.00 per year or $8.34 per month is worth it to the homeowners to transfer the risk of flash floods.

This example was oversimplified, however, it can help you understand the concept of an insurance transfer by showing the relationship between the premium paid and the payment of loss. In reality, of course, the insurance company would be dealing with thousands of risks. The rate making process is highly complicated, and takes in numerous factors such as profit, expenses, competition, and regulations. The bottom line, however, is that insurance companies collect huge amounts of data in order to provide a statistically reliable rate. And from this standpoint the homeowners of Eagan Minnesota are able to pay the predictable premium instead of the potentially large, unknown amount that a flash flood might bring. Simply stated, insurance is the transfer of risk from an insured to an insurance company, where numerous like insured people are all pooled together. Each insured person pays a small fixed cost or premium, in return for the pledge of a larger, unknown payment or claim, in the event of a loss.

If you wish to get a loan from a bank for a building, your inventory, or a vehicle, you must have evidence that it's insured and that the bank is also named on the insurance policy. Banks have a belief that if a person loses something and no longer has the benefit of something then they have a tendency to not pay for the item. The reason this is done is that the property is used as collateral for the loan. If fire or some other peril destroys the building and its contents, the collateral for the loan is also destroyed. Insurance provides protection so that the bank can be repaid for the value of the loan even though the collateral was destroyed. Insurance is an important part of credit around the world, since without it banks wouldn't take the risks involved in making loans. Without loans fewer people would be able to get enough capital together to open their own business. Fewer businesses mean fewer jobs and even fewer people able to get capital together. I did get a loan for two acres of undeveloped land with only $1,000 down. No insurance and the land was the collateral. Not much can happen to land so the bank said, "I didn't need any insurance to secure the loan."

Insurance enables business people to use their capital more efficiently. By paying a fixed premium or known cost, people are able to budget their business expenses. Without insurance protection, business people could face a large outlay of cash after an uninsured loss. Like some of the people of Eagan Minnesota learned in the flash flood last July. Because a businessperson knows what their insurance premium is, they can plan to use cash on hand for the growth and development of the small business.

Insurance companies provide loss control and loss prevention assistance as a service to their insured people. These services include helping maintain a healthy work atmosphere for you and your employees, thereby increasing production and employee satisfaction. They also give advice as how to prevent loss of life, like they might say not to go surfing or swimming in a drainage ditch during a flash flood because you might get sucked into a water pipe and drown. Don't store gasoline in your kitchen's oven. Don't stick your hand under a lawnmower while it's running. Yet people do these things all the time. Every year in Minnesota somebody falls through the ice and at least one-person sticks his or her hand in a snow blower to try and free up the stuck snow. Every single year without fail somebody gets hurt doing something without thinking. Insurance companies also assist business owners in developing efficient methods of loss control to help prevent accidents, injuries, and higher premiums.

One of the biggest and most important advantages of insurance is the feeling of security it provides. You might not be thinking that, as your writing out the check for the premium but you'll feel that way if you ever have to cash an insurance check to make up for lost goods. Insurance is a promise from the insurance company to pay in the event of a loss. Such a promise decreases the uncertainty involved in a risk. You're going to put a considerable amount of time and money into starting a new small business; insurance helps to provide you with the feeling that your investment will be protected in the event of an unforeseen catastrophe. Even if you haven't used the insurance money for a loss, the money has not been wasted. Insurance has allowed you to take a risk of starting a new business and to continue to have a business develop and grow, without insurance the threat of catastrophe loss constantly is over your head. Insurance is the greatest protection a small business can have.

Before you first start a new small business, you should know you need protection, however, you also need somebody to help you put together the correct insurance program that would adequately protect your business assets. Like some of the homeowners of Eagan Minnesota found out after the flash flood. First you have to decide whether you want to deal with an agent or a broker.

There are two types of agents, independent agent and direct writers. An independent agent is one that represents one or more insurance companies, anywhere from one to thirty. The agent is an independent businessperson who has a contract with each company for which he or she sells insurance. The insurance agent collects the relevant information from a business or homeowner, evaluates it, and then selects the most appropriate insurance company for the purchaser's needs. One advantage of using an independent agent is that such an agent has several sources from which to select the best coverage for a client. An independent agent can change from one insurance company to another if such a move appears to be beneficial to the insured.

A direct writer is an agent that represents only one insurance company, usually because they strongly believe in that company. When a small business owner purchases coverage through a direct writer, the agent places the business with one company that he or she represents. The agent may be a salaried representative of the insurance company or the insurance company may have an exclusive contract preventing the agent from representing any other insurance company. One possible advantage of using a direct writer, as an agent is that, because of the exclusive relationship between the agent and the insurance company, the cost of the insurance may be lower than would be the case with a company using the independent agent. Therefore, any savings could be passed on to the consumer in the form of lower premiums.

In developing an insurance program, a business owner may also deal with an insurance broker. A broker differs from an agent in that an agent represents a company or companies, whereas a broker represents the insured, and attempts to locate an insurance company willing to write coverage for the insured's business. A broker can provide a more flexible market for the insured's needs, because a broker is free to search out a wide variety of insurance companies to serve the insured. Brokers can also save you money.

Once an agent or broker gathers the information needed for an insurance quote, he or she submits it to the insurance company. An independent or broker may submit an application to several insurance companies. At the company, underwriters evaluate the information and determine whether it's the type of risk they're interested in writing. If it's acceptable to the company, the underwriter will then have a premium developed based on the rate that have been formulated for that type of risk. Credits or debits may be added to these rates depending on the different characteristics of each application submitted. The insurance company returns the premium quote and application coverage to the agent or broker, who then presents them to the business or homeowner. The homeowner or business owner can either accept or reject the quote.

Another example, on July 12, 2000 at about 10:30AM somebody broke into two of the cars at Rasmussen College in Eagan Minnesota. Out of one truck they stole a purse and a laptop computer, out of the second car they stole a pack of cigarettes. That's right they broke a $189.00 window for a pack of cigarettes. Both cars were parked beside each other and no more than three steps apart. The college is not responsible for this crime but if the people who own the cars have insurance they should be covered. Funny how I'm writing about insurance and all these really good examples come up, I'm glad I'm not writing about tornados. To finish the flash flood in Eagan Minnesota, the federal government declared the flash flood a disaster and plans on giving victims federal aid.

Since the insurance company's only part of a contract is the promise to pay in the event of a loss, as a business owner you should be concerned with the background and financial stability of the company that handles your insurance coverage. Before making a final decision, therefore, you should get as much information as possible concerning the insurance company and its background, its size, and its claims-paying history. An insurance agent, the state insurance department, or an independent rating source such as Dun & Bradstreet or Best's Insurance Rating can supply such information. Best's provides several ratings for most insurance companies. Letter notations (A, B, C) are used to indicate the financial stability and claims-paying ability of each company.

> Bet you Insurance Company
> Established——1989
> Claims-Paying Ability—A+
> Financial Stability——-A+
> Reserves——-$3,000,000,000

In addition to financial stability and claims-paying ability of the insurance company, there are several other factors to consider in choosing an insurance agent. Service is the key to any insurance program. Good service from both the company and the agent should be a top priority, since insurance is a service business and their only asset to you is the promise to pay your claim if something should go wrong. However, an insurance agent is like a lawyer. An insured person must feel comfortable with an agent and a company, and have confidence that they can, and if necessary, will do the job of keeping the promise to pay.

Insurance is an extremely complicated subject that's constantly changing. I've looked at and looked into insurance about as hard as a person can look into it and ask questions about insurance with out completely upsetting the unlucky agent who I interviewed for this book. Not to lose my creditability but as an insurance buyer it's up to you to stay alert to these changes in the industry. There are brand new crimes being committed every day. Just some in the last few years were computer crimes, stealing ID's, and hackers. There are new crimes and new disasters coming up all the time now. Sometimes insurance agents don't know all the new things happening. There are some professionals out there who can help. CIC-Certified Insurance Counselors, CPCU-Chartered Property and Casualty Underwriter, AAI-Accredited Advisor in Insurance, and ARM-Associate in Risk Management.

The cost of a product and service is always important. Much more important to most thoughtful consumers, though, is whether the value is worth the price. As with any purchase, the cheapest insurance is not always the best buy. You must take all the factors just discussed into account in determining the real value purchased with the premium paid. Insurance premiums are a business expense and can be written off.

Although each insurance company may use its own form of insurance policy, most policies will contain the same basic elements and have the same basic structure. Many companies subscribe to and use forms developed by the Insurance Service Office or "ISO", a nonprofit corporation that makes available to insurance companies information concerning ratings, statistics, actuarial data, and policy forms. By using the information and policy forms developed by ISO, policies are more standardized. This enables an insurance company to save money by not having to develop its own policy forms and dig out its own rating information. It also benefits the insurance consumer by making it easier to compare insurance policies. With some exceptions, most ISO policies and other company policies will have the same basic characteristics we'll discuss in this book.

Property consists of real property and personal property. Real property is land and improvements upon land, such as buildings and other structures. Unimproved land is generally not insurable and like I said earlier I bought land via loan and the bank didn't demand that I have insurance on it. Personal property is any property other than real property as defined above, such as furniture, money, and business inventory. The loss of income to a business due to the destruction of real property is the subject of property insurance.

A peril is a cause of loss. There are numerous perils that may cause a loss to property. Some of the most common ones are listed here.

Fire: When many people think of insurance coverage, they think first of protection from a fire loss. Fire, is an important peril to insure against, is a common coverage in almost all property policies.

Lightning: Can cause severe damage even if it doesn't start a fire. Lightning doesn't have to make a direct hit to interrupt the flow of business.

Vandalism: One of the perils that's neither a natural cause nor an act of God. Vandalism, however, is a major problem in some areas of the country. Mostly graffiti.

Explosions: Boilers or gas lines are examples of this type of destruction that can cause damage to a building and its contents.

Here's a list of things to insure against smoke, hailstorms, windstorms, falling objects, vehicles, water or flood, ice and snow, sprinkler leakage, earthquakes, sinkhole collapse, and the big one theft of property.

Citizens in this country have certain legally protected rights as a result of common law, its judicial interpretations, and statutes. Your customers have the right to expect you to maintain safe and hazard-free small businesses. When such a right exists, there's an obligation to respect that right on the part of the other person. If that right is violated, the injured party may bring suit to recover for damages. A violation of the right of another party is a legal wrong. It can be either criminal wrong or a civil wrong.

A criminal wrong results in criminal action being brought against the wrongdoer. Examples of criminal wrongs are assault and battery, murder, rape, and theft. State governments have statues that set forth the elements of each crime and the details of its punishment. Criminal wrongs are generally not insurable, however, in robbery cases the store maybe able to file a claim to recover the money stolen.

A civil wrong arises from the breach of a duty owed to a member of the public. The wronged party subjects a person or organization that breaches this duty to an action for damages. An example of this is the beating of a suspect in Philadelphia Pennsylvania, the Philadelphia police beat a man after he shot another policeman in the hand and tried to get away in a police car. After the police finally caught the criminal all seven of the policemen started to beat on him. Civil wrongs can be based on either contracts or torts. If one party fails to perform its obligations to contract and this failure leads to injury or damages to another party, legal action maybe brought against the liable party. This is contractual liability. With a contract, the obligations of one party to another are voluntarily assumed.

A tort is a wrongful act, other than contractual, that violates a person's rights. The three forms of tort are intentional liability, absolute liability, and negligence. Intentional liability includes any intentional bodily injury, personal injury, or property damage, like trespassing, libel, and slander. If you intentionally slander a competitor, they may sue for intentional tort. Absolute or strict liability is that liability imposed by law without any negligence or intent by the liable party. Example, if you had a vicious watchdog on the premises and it got lose and bit somebody coming into your store to buy something, You maybe sued for tort absolute or strict liability. Negligence is the failure to exercise reasonable care to another party, which results in injuries or damage. Reasonable care is usually considered to mean the type of care a prudent and ordinary person would take in the same situation. This is similar to the philosophy of Immanual Kant's duty based philosophy on ethics, which I've talked about in my books "Olivononics and Olivononics Two". A court of law decides whether reasonable care was indeed being exercised. An example of negligence would be keeping a loaded gun behind the counter in case you get robbed. The gun goes off hurting or killing somebody you maybe sued for negligence. Lawyers live and love suing people and better yet businesses for negligence tort.

Insurance is to business what a heart is to the human body. To run a business without insurance is like running across a tight rope blindfolded and without a safety net. It's like betting everything you own on one roll of the dice. Never consider going without some kind of insurance to protect your new small business. Include insurance expenses in your business plans. Insurance premiums are tax deductible and can be written off as an expense for you small business.

Chapter Four

Getting the Money

When starting your business, you'll need two types of accounts to make the company work: start-up capital and working capital. You'll use the start-up capital to get the doors open, rent or mortgage, utility deposits, office supplies, office equipment, and insurance and legal fee payments. A small business loan from your local bank is a good way to get your capital.

When you make a request for a loan, the bank is going to look at how practical your approach is, both to your business and to your loan request. A bank lends money based on well-secured and well-conceived business plans, which plainly demonstrate the ability to repay the loan. In other words, banks need to know up front if you can pay back the loan. Since the bank has to justify making your loan to its loan committee, to its board of directors, and to its bank examiner, it must have a sound documentation in the form of a well thought out business plan. Remember, a bank doesn't lend money on the basis of your appearance and personality; it makes loans on the probability of making money from the loan. Many good business ventures fail because the owner had a poorly prepared loan request, and no working plan to show the bank how the proposed business plans to pay back the loan. Even if you have more than enough collateral to cover the loan request, you still need to present a good business plan.

The bank doesn't want your home or assets, and the ugliness of a foreclosure procedure; it's in the business of loaning money for a fee. They'll take your assets only if they feel there's no other logical way of recovering the money from a loan. Banks will also make arrangements to help you get caught up on a loan if you fall behind. However this is only done as a last resort and normally only done a few times in the beginning of the business. Never take advantage of the banks willingness to help string out the payments. During your coarse of business you will more than likely need their help again and they simply will refuse to help. If you really do need some ideas to help your business if it's falling behind, a bank may give you some business ideas. Nevertheless, the problem is your problem and not the banks. If, however, it does become the banks problem: do to your incompetence, the bank will solve only their end of the problem.

The rate of interest charge is a predetermined number of points, commonly known as percentage points, over the current prime interest rate. The prime rate is the interest rate set by individual banks for their largest, low risk loans, usually short term unsecured credit to veterans, creditworthy customers. Just as in any business, a bank marks up the prime rate to cover its overhead and to make a profit for its stockholders.

This is not just a small business management book, it's also a philosophy book, as a member of the "APPA" American Philosophical Practitioners Association, I find the urge to talk philosophically too overwhelming to resist. Plus I feel that more business managers would be better off learning some philosophical out looks. As individuals, the only thing that we own is our beliefs. If you believe something to be true, you consider it to be your knowledge. If, however, you don't believe something to be true, you have very little knowledge of it. So knowledge is power but only if you believe it to be true. If, for example, a bank believes your plan to be true, then to the best of his or her knowledge, beliefs, your plan will work and he or she will loan you the money. If, however, he or she doesn't believe your business plan will work, he or she will have very little knowledge of your business plans. I'm truly afraid that it's that simple my friends. When you go to a bank for a loan, plan on meeting a well-seasoned veteran at looking at business plans. Lets start with working capital.

Working capital consists of the money needed to operate a business for the first 30 to 90 days until sales or service are being made and cash is coming in. It's easy to underestimate the amount of working capital you'll need because of the existence of what are called, "Hidden or unknown costs." Yes, unexpected bummers can eat away at the working capital like a bunch of piranha. You should therefore make some kind of allowance for these hidden costs. One way to do this is to include a contingency fund in your estimate of working capital requirements. The myth that banks don't like to see allowances is not true. A bank will not frown on such allowances for hidden costs; on the contrary, it will view the request as reflecting as honest and practical approach to business realities, especially if this is your first venture in small business.

A critical factor in determining the amount of working capital needed is your business credit plan. If your business is strictly cash & carry, then you'll probably need enough to cover 30 days of operating expenses. If, however, you plan on extending 30 days credit to your customers, then you would probably need 60 days of operating expenses. In fact because of the hidden and unknown expenses, it probably wouldn't be a bad idea to ask the bank for three months of operating expenses.

All new business will have hidden and unexpected bummers in your start-up. The more thoroughly you research a new business venture, the less likely you are to have unpleasant surprises in the form of costs you hadn't expected. Remember, all the research you do in advance costs nothing but your time. All the unexpected bummers cost you nothing but money and working capital.

Research can consist of talking to everybody you think you'll be involved with, including prospective landlords, competitors, suppliers, a good accountant, and even prospective customers, if at all possible. In general, people are usually willing to talk about business. Also, most people are flattered when you ask for their advice, and are willing to try to answer almost any business related questions. In fact take notes on what the other people have told you, it could come in handy when constructing your operating expenses list, which you're going to show the bank when asking for a loan.

There are various types of lenders among which the small businessperson can choose. The first and most common source of funds is family and friends. Those already familiar with your character and personality are often less intimidating to approach for money than a stranger at a lending institution, and sometimes these sources can be used very successfully. However, any agreements you make with friends or family members must be put into writing and signed by all parties involved. It's strongly recommended that you use an attorney to draft a proper agreement. Such agreements can save grief and bad feelings later on, and even avoid possible litigations. People have a tendency to forget the terms of an oral agreement, or to misunderstand the terms to begin with. One must first look to understand before you can be understood. When both parties sign an agreement, a contract is formed. If necessary, you can always amend the agreement later on with the consent of all other parties involved.

It's also important to realize that anybody who lends you money literally becomes your partner. Whether that investor works with you on a day-to-day basis or simply invests in your company as a nonworking partner, the role of the investor must be clearly defined before one single dollar changes hands. Many friends and families have been ruined due because of poor communications over money. Some people will make financial commitments with people they know on a handshake, with nothing in writing. Verbal agreements are fine to begin with but before any money changes hands a written agreement must be formed. The handshakes should be delayed until after you have a written agreement understood and signed by all parties involved. No Exceptions!

In addition to family and friends, you might want to consider taking on a business partner at the outset of your business. A partner can provide great assistance in managing and financing of your business. Normally, a partner owns one half of the company, provide he or she puts in one half of the money. There are many variations to this format. A partner might only put in 40% of the money while you put the other 60% and thereby retain control of the company. Whatever ratio is agreed upon becomes the profit and loss participation ratio as well. You may also consider taking a partner with little or no money but is extremely talented and knows your business. Regardless of what arrangements you decide upon, have a written agreement clearly spelling out the duties and responsibilities of everybody involved. Again, you can easily amend the agreement at a later date, if you want the responsibilities change. It's also very sound business advice to review such agreements at least once per year and more if need be.

Commercial banks are generally regarded as the most cost-effective source of financing for small businesses. Only banks can borrow money from the Federal Reserve, and therefore take advantage of current prime rates. Commercial banks usually make short-term or intermediate loans of up to five years to most small businesses, depending on how much collateral the business or individual has.

All banks have certain lending characteristics that are fairly easy to determine and understand. For example, many banks prefer to lend to certain types of businesses. Thus, Bank Royal may specialize in "floor planning" used car operations that bank Myers wouldn't even consider doing. Before you begin to actively seek a loan, find out exactly what types of businesses a given bank prefers to deal with. You can get this information from any lending officer of the bank via a simple telephone call.

How should you actually go about picking the right bank for your business? First place you should look is the bank that you're already dealing with. This way the banks can search their own records to see what kind of risk or safe bet that you are. Interview the people at the banks as you would interview a prospective accountant. Get recommendations from lawyers, your accountant, other trusted business owners, and other bankers. Visit each bank under consideration, and ask questions. Be open-mined.

Open-mindedness is the key to understanding what your getting into as well as to help you decide on the perfect situation for you and your business. Many people speak of being open-minded, however, unfortunately, most people proclaim to be open-minded because it sounds really cool and is socially acceptable. I believe that open-mindedness is somewhat beyond the grasp of the adverage individual. In order to understand open-mindedness we must first seek to understand so that I "We" can be understood. My definition of open-mindedness is that in order for you to consider yourself open-minded, you simply have to be willing to consider anything and everything. Whether or not you agree with it is beside the point. There's a myth that says, "If you say no to a premise or a proposition, you're not open-minded." No, this isn't true, if you consider the proposition or premise and disagree with it, you're still open-minded because you considered it in the first place. If, however, you're unwilling to even hear or consider an idea or proposition, you are not open-minded. I'm personally about 99% open-minded, which means there are a few things that I'm unwilling to consider. Bank robbery or murder for example.

Of primary concern, of coarse, is the selection of a bank that's financially sound, that follows established commercial banking practices, and that has a reputation for customer satisfaction. You should also investigate the bank's services and methods of operation. Is the bank federally insured? Is its management experienced? Does it offer the services that you need? Does it offer the services you may need five or ten years from now? Does it have the assets to handle the largest loan your company is likely to require? Are its key personnel easy to deal with? If you're dealing in used cars, furniture, major appliances, or other items that customers usually buy on time, will the bank assist these customers in financing such purchases? Can they, if needed, help set up and administer a pension fund, profit sharing, and payroll deductions for the IRS? Yes, some banks will even offer to handle payroll for you. Banks are discovering that such managerial assistance is a vital part of managing a successful small business loan portfolio.

Before making a final decision as to which commercial bank to approach, shop around. Lending policies of small banks with less than 20-million in deposits vary dramatically from the policies of large banks with over 100-million in deposits. Again, these policies may be affected by the nature of your business. The best way to find out the lending policies of any bank is to ask one of its lending officers about the bank's requirements. They're usually eager to help or turn you in the right direction.

When approaching a commercial bank for a loan, you should be aware of current interest rates or at least have an idea. If rates are low, banks usually have an abundance of money to lend and are more aggressive in their lending policies. On the other hand, if rates are high and the demand for money is great, banks tend to be very much more selective in their lending policies, lending only to the best prospects with the most tempting loan application packages. It's supply and demand just like any other business.

Generally speaking, there are three basic types of commercial bank loans: Short, intermediate, and long-term. Short-term loans are loans available for a term of up to a year. Usually the easiest kind of loan to obtain, you can get one for almost any reason. For example, most businesses are seasonal. During peak months of the year, such businesses use short-term loans to finance additional inventory requirements. Also, a bank requires less in the way of documentation on short-term loans, and they're consequently less expensive for the bank to process. In addition, the bank is aware that in the course of repaying a short-term loan, a business is less likely to undergo the kind of radical changes that might get it into serious financial trouble.

A short-term loan is an excellent way to establish a good track record with your bank, and thereby increasing your borrowing power. For example, suppose your business is really starting to click and cash is rolling in. You might consider asking for a 30-day loan for additional inventory during your peak period. If you pay off the loan on the due date, you have proven to the bank that your company is a good risk for a short-term loan. Not only are you increasing your credibility but you're also developing a track record of reliability with your bank. A sound track record will help you if you have to deal with another bank for any reason too. Banks report your credit rating to the credit bureau.

A common practice for banks today is to ask for a personal guarantee on short-term loans even if the business is incorporated. A personal guarantee requires you to use your personal assets as security. Some businesspeople find this policy objectionable; remember, that banks are in the business to make money, and they're simply trying to protect its investment in your company. I personally don't feel a personal guarantee is going to do any good. Banks somehow do.

If one side of the coin says, "Man has no guarantees in life." Then it's safe to assume that the opposite side of the coin guarantees man one thing, "No individual can live forever." Yet, it's not difficult to find somebody willing to flip the coin in search of a guarantee. The guarantee they usually find isn't very satisfying. I guarantee it.

Intermediate loans are from three to five years long. As you can guess they are a little harder to obtain than short-term loans. The bank will require a completely documented justification when you apply for such a loan. You would consider an intermediate loan in order to buy equipment, like machinery, or such long-term assets as buildings. These items become collateral to the loan, which in turn offers the bank additional security.

A long-term loan is generally a loan granted for a period in excess of five years. Most banks don't look favorably on long-term loans for small business. Don't get me wrong; a bank will make an exception for real estate purchases, or for the construction of a business facilities. The bank will demand to become the mortgage holder or the first trust-deed holder of the property.

When you take out a long-term business loan with a bank, the bank will usually require an ongoing financial update on your business, often in the form of financial statements, like income statements or balance sheets. In addition, a bank officer will probably visit your facility periodically to see how the business is progressing. Since bank officers are very good at sizing up a business in the course of such visits, you should have your company as orderly and well organized as possible when a bank officer visits your business. Remember, you want the bank always to see your company in the best possible way.

When business is going well, invite your banker to your place of business and show him or her exactly how you're using the bank's money. Be open to your banker's suggestions. Remember, your banker has your best interest at heart since those interests are also the bank's. In addition, a good banker wants to have a cordial and ongoing relationship with the bank's clients and successful business owners.

If you're applying for a long-term business loan, the bank will usually require you to prepare extensive documentation. It's a good idea to read every line of every page of every loan document from the bank. Have your lawyer review all bank documents as well. You can never be too careful.

In addition to the three basic types of loans, there are other financing techniques you might like to try or consider. There's accounts receivable financing, which is a type of loan available from commercial banks. Under this arrangement, you put up as collateral a portion of your accounts receivable and the bank will lend you about 70 to 80 percent of its value. You need not pledge all your receivables but only enough to cover the amount of the loan. Pledge enough so that after the bank discounts their value by 20 to 30 percent, you have enough left to cover your requirements on the loan. When looking for a bank to use, inquire as to whether it offers accounts receivable financing or not. Banks are usually looking to wheel and deal.

Another idea to get some money together is called, "Factoring." Factoring is by far the last alternative method that I can think of for borrowing money. In a factoring arrangement, the bank buys your accounts receivable outright and assumes the responsibility of collecting the debt. You can remove the receivables from your ledger as soon as the arrangement with the bank is made, increasing the cash value of your business accordingly. The bank will charge interest on the money from the time it buys the receivables until the time it collects them. In addition, the bank will usually charge a service fee amounting to fix percentage of the receivables involved.

In the next chapters that follow, we're going to look at philosophy because I believe that a well-rounded individual will do better as a business entrepreneur than somebody who's never studied philosophy. Together we're going to learn about the human mind, business ethics, reality, and business logic. Understanding reality will also help you market better than the adverage individual. Please keep an open-mind when reading from this point on.

Marketing and advertising are basically using philosophy of what you believe to be true of the human mind to sell your product or service to make a living. If you can get people to believe that they need your product or service, then you can expect them to buy. If, however, you cannot get them to believe in your product or service they will have no knowledge of your business and will not buy. There is no universal right and wrong in marketing or advertising but only what individuals believe that will work. If you believe something to be true, you consider it to be your knowledge. If you don't believe something to be true, you have no knowledge of what to do. Books on marketing and advertising are nothing more than people's philosophy on what they believe will help you make more sells or your product or service. So now we are going to look at the human mind in a philosophical manner to see if we can create a marketing or advertising philosophy to get customers to buy your product or service.

Chapter Five

Understanding the Human Mind

What is the human mind? Is it physical or non-physical? Is the mind separate from the brain or is it part of the brain? In order for us to learn how to think like a philosopher; we must first try and look at the human mind. In this chapter I'm going to look at some of the basic philosophies of the human mind and see if we can learn how to philosophically look at the questions of the mind. Today we have scientists looking at the mind as well. We live in a time when mad gunmen have shooting sprees whenever they feel like it. So it's important for science to understand the human mind. That science is called Psychology.

Philosophy of the mind is different than psychology. Psychology is a science of studying human behavior and thought. It's based on observation of people often under controlled experimental conditions. Social psychology is the study of how the mind gets along in society. Philosophy of the mind isn't an experimental or an observation of a scientific experiment. Philosophy instead concentrates on the analysis of our concepts. Philosophers are concerned with conceptual issues that come up when talking about the mind. How do you view your mind? Is it possible that a scientist could study your mind?

A psychologist would investigate a personality disorder by examining the patients or by running tests on them. A philosopher would ask conceptual questions like, "What is the mind?" or "What is mental illness?" These questions can't be answered by observing other people. It requires the philosopher to analyze the meaning of the term in which they're expressed. How can somebody else say that somebody is mentally ill? Who's to say that a certain person is mentally ill? The person who we claim to be ill might be the only one who's sane. How do we know who is in their right mind? People thought Noah was crazy for building the ark.

In order for us to think like a philosopher we must be open minded about what other people believe to be true. A person has a belief about something because they ream it to be true until proven otherwise. A narrow-minded person will still believe their philosophies even if there is overwhelming evidence to prove otherwise. Some people are concerned in their image more than finding out if a new belief is true or not. A person who's constantly changing their opinions about their beliefs gives the impression of being constantly unstable. It's like the person doesn't believe in his or her own beliefs, which give the illusion of being unstable and uncertain about a belief or plans for the future. Is a person who changes their beliefs or plans really unstable? Is another person's philosophy that contradicts your philosophy always wrong? Should you convince the other person why they're wrong or should you look at their new view with an opened mind? Is it possible to convince somebody of anything?

In 1492, Columbus sailed the ocean blue and discovered America. Well right after the Indians did and proved the world was round. That would be like somebody discovering money in my pocket. Before Columbus discovered America people thought the world was flat. To the best of their beliefs the world was as flat as a table. I can understand why they thought that. If I would stand on an ocean beach and look out to sea it would appear to drop off or end. Can you find any adult in America that truly believes that the world is flat? Do you believe the world is round? Did you build a space ship and fly into space to look down at the earth and say, "Yep looks round to me." Did you pay thousands of dollars to go on a cruise to make sure the world was round? People have been on around the world cruises but not to make sure the world was in fact round. So it's a universal assumption that the world is round. The same universal assumption that was made before 1492, that the world was in fact flat.

By questioning your own beliefs you're starting to think like a philosopher. Do you believe in God? How did you come to that belief? Did you adopt that belief from somebody else? Did you reason it out for yourself of why you have that belief or it's a universal knowledge that everybody knows and should never question? If it's a universal knowledge that should never be questioned than what certainty do we have on it? If the world is flat is a universal knowledge that should never be questioned, then how could mankind ever have found out that the world is round? If you have beliefs that are never questioned then how do you know them to be true? In order to think like a philosopher, you must question even your own beliefs. I'm going to look at some of the fundamentals of philosophies of the human mind and see if we can try and think of the human mind as a philosopher would.

There is a mind body connection problem that philosophers enjoy arguing over. The first philosophy is called Dualism. Dualism believes that the mind is separate from the body and can continue on after death. While a person is alive it's called the mind and after the person is dead it's called the spirit or soul. A tractor-trailer has dual wheels if one of the tires goes flat the other tire will go on and support the truck. Dualism helps explain the fact that there is life after death and the mind does go on living even though the body is dead. The only way the mind can go on after death is if it's separate from the body. If the mind weren't separate from the body then the mind would have to go with the body into death. Which would be the same existence you were in before you were born. Most religions support the dualism philosophy.

Physicalists believe that the mind is not separate from the body and that the mind and body are one in the same. Physicalists do not believe in life after death. The only way a physicalist could believe in life after death is if they would consider the resurrection of somebody who's already dead. If the mind and body are one and the same then both must go into death together and both must come out of death together. If you believe that both mind and body are the same then there is no both but only one. To a physicalist the mind might be electrical impulses shooting down nerve endings to represent thinking. Electric is a physical thing. So is the electric running in our outlets thinking about how to run the appliances in our house? So when I turn a switch on I'm bringing something like thinking back to life? A physicalist would say there are many different types of electrical impulses and the impulses in your mind could be thinking. We have a science and know that the body uses electric impulses to make body parts move. Even if a person is dead we can shock them and make the dead body move.

A Dualist would then argue well I'm not questioning if electric can make muscles move but I'm questioning the fact that does the mind use electric impulses to move the body. Where do these electric impulses come from? What is flipping the switches on and off? What is making the electric to shoot down the nerve endings in the first place? When I'm driving a car I use the gas pedal and the brake I steer the car and I use the car as a way to get around. I'm a living thing using a physical thing to get around. So is the mind driving my body around using electrical impulses? The mind is a living thing using a physical thing to get around in. The mind is in fact using the body to benefit the mind while the body is alive. Can you hold a mind in your hand or only the physical thing, which houses the mind, called the brain?

A physicalist would ask, "If the mind can go on after death where is it before we are born?" If something has a beginning then it must also have an end as well. If something is not physical then it's spiritual and you have no way to prove your theory. Nobody ever proved they could talk to a spirit. If two people would try and drive a car together, one steering and one working the pedals, is it possible for two separate beings to work in such harmony to drive a car? Then somebody is driving a car they work alone. That means in order to have such harmony they must be one because two separate beings couldn't work in such harmony together. We have evidence that proves electrical impulses move the body. Nobody has proof that there's life after death. We don't know as of yet where the electrical impulses come from but in time hopefully we will. We learn something new every day maybe will learn why tomorrow.

Can you see the arguments on the mind body connection? Which do you believe and why? In order to think like a philosopher you must look at all the arguments on both sides. Is life after death possible? When we die is that all they wrote for us? Do we go back into the same existence we where in before we were born? Do we go on to collect our just rewards? Does believing in life after death, make us feel better about our own death? Can you picture what it would be like to go back into the same existence you where in before you where born? Is there anyway to answer this question and be sure that you're right? Until somebody comes along with written in stone hardcore evidence then the philosopher must take a stand on what they believe to be true. Things that you believe to be true are referred to as knowledge. So to the best of your knowledge you believe what you do or to the best of your beliefs. What do you think of this?

Blaise Pascal (1623-1662) made the famous Pascal's Wager. It goes something like this. If I wager for God, and God exists. Than I'll have infinite gains. Not only will I live a righteous life but will get rewarded in the after life. If I wager for God, and God does not exist. Than I've still lived a righteous life. If I wager against God and God does exists. Than I'll have infinite loss, pain, and suffering but I could've lived life anyway that I choose to. If I wager against God and God does not exist. Than I can live life however I felt like or could get away with and suffered no losses. This wager isn't for the weak hearted. Yet almost everybody make or takes the Pascal's wager. If you wager for God then which God is it? Should you wager on the Jewish religion or the Christian religion? If God does exist God would only take souls in the right religion. To think like a philosopher you must sometimes take a stand in what you believe to be true to the best of your beliefs or knowledge. Some issues will take a lifetime to come to a conclusion on. This wager is one of great conceptual value to consider.

Some people believe that we have a subconscious mind. So it's safe to assume that we have a conscious mind. The conscious mind is who we are but the subconscious mind demands justice and possibly makes us feel guilty when we've done something wrong. So if you believe in the subconscious mind is it possible to have two minds in one brain? If the subconscious mind is different than the conscious mind then in fact we have two minds in one brain. Could the other mind that we refer to as the subconscious mind, in fact be a whole different mind from ours all together? Did you ever hear somebody say, "Something's telling me not to do that." Could that something be a completely different mind telling us "No" or giving us a second opinion? Is the subconscious mind there to guide us through life? These are conceptual questions on the subconscious mind. How could a philosopher answer these questions? Let's see if we can.

Were not sure where the minds come from or where the mind goes before or after life. The sperm cell fertilizes the egg and makes a baby. The sperm cell is one organ and the egg is one organ. So we have two separate organs combining together to make one human being. So if were combing two to make one is it possible to combine two minds into one brain? The sperm might have had one mind. The egg might have had one mind. When they combined together it could give the baby two minds. One mind being a conscious mind and the other being a subconscious mind. So is it possible for the sperm's mind to be our conscious mind and the egg's mind to be our subconscious mind? Do we have control over our subconscious mind? Is our conscious mind the subconscious mind to our other mind? Is there another mind in our brain that perceives our conscious mind, as it's subconscious mind? Let's put this in perspective.

Let's say we have two people in a car. The car is going to be considered to be our body. The driver is going to be considered our conscious mind and the person in the back seat of the car is going to be considered our subconscious mind. The driver of our body is going to be our conscious mind and doesn't have any control over what the other mind says in the back seat. The mind in the back seat is paying attention to what the driver is doing. Every now and then the mind in the back seat will say slow down or I saw what you did. The mind in the back seat cannot drive the car but can say anything it wants. We can only control our conscious mind but we have to listen to all that the subconscious mind wants to say. The subconscious mind could also keep score on all the wrong things you do and demand justice for your wrong doings.

In order for you to think like a philosopher you must adopt this philosophy as your own or criticize my philosophy. Do you agree with the sperm and egg philosophy of both having their own mind? Why do you think we have two separate minds? Do you think it's only one mind but appears to be two? To criticize the philosophy you could say, "What about twins? Twins develop when the egg splits in two after it's been fertilized. So does both minds split as well? Each twin will have a subconscious as well as a conscious mind. If both minds split then it should be a copy of the original so the twins would think alike. Yet the twins don't think alike so why is a mind that splits into two end up thinking differently than it's twin?" To support my philosophy I could say, " Both twins do think alike but because of different external world encounters the mind adapted to it's own private situations. Both minds might not have encountered the same situations as the other so they must adapt differently which gives the illusion of not thinking the same way." Here again you must adopt this philosophy or criticize it or invent your own philosophy on the subconscious mind. The only way to answer this conceptual question is with hard cord scientific evidence. So until then we the philosophers will argue the issue.

Does the subconscious mind demand justice for our wrong doings? Is somebody throwing a fit, trying to justify some wrong doing that they've committed? Is the subconscious mind responsible for giving us feelings of guilt? Where do you think guilty feelings come from within our minds? Let's say that a man rapes a woman and gets convicted on the rape and goes to prison. If we ask the woman, what should the rapist's punishment be? She might say, "I think he should be in constant torment in this life and beyond or given the death penalty." In the criminal's subconscious mind he might agree with the victim and think he should be in constant torment in this life and beyond. The criminal could be sitting in prison and having a good day. The criminal's subconscious mind might not think that he's in torment enough so it'll demand justice to try and balance out his wrong doings of raping the woman. So for no apparent reason the criminal will break a prison rule and force the prison to make it harder on the criminal. Since things are now harder on the criminal and he's in more torment the subconscious mind now has a better feeling of balance because now both the criminal as well as the victim are in agreement that the criminal should be in constant torment in this life and possible beyond. If you would ask the criminal why did you break the rule for no apparent reason? The criminal might answer, "I have no idea why." The criminal himself may not know the answer.

In order for you to think like a philosopher you must adopt this philosophy as your own or criticize the philosophy or invent your own on the subconscious mind's quest for justice. By questioning this philosophy you might be able to come up with your own philosophy on the subconscious mind. Is the subconscious mind away of balancing out our wrong doings? If a man is unstable enough to rape a woman then it shouldn't be surprising that he acts like a fool in prison as well. Raping a woman is not the sign of a stable mind. Therefore why should we expect him to act right in prison? Is it possible to try and balance out our wrong doings in the subconscious mind with out consciously knowing that's why we are acting the way we are? Is the subconscious mind deceitful to our conscious mind in its quest for balance? Is it possible for us to not know why we did a certain act or say something we shouldn't have? What do you think is true about the subconscious mind so far? What argument do you have against my views?

Let's say we have two brothers, one's named Mike and the other Billy. Mike is an honor role student and is dating an attractive woman and Billy is not doing well in school and doesn't have any friends. Let's say that Billy bad mouths his brother's girlfriend and criticizes Mike's honor role achievements but doesn't really have a reason to do so. Mike might even ask, "Billy why are you criticizing my honor role at school and bad mouthing my girlfriend?" Billy might say, "I don't know why." First thing to come to mind is the fact that Billy might be jealous of Mike. What exactly is jealousy? To think like a philosopher you must not just assume and label an act as jealousy or rage you must think of the conceptual questions to answer for yourself of why Billy is acting mean for no apparent reason. Is Billy's subconscious mind trying to get balance by downing Mike so that Billy and Mike feel like they're on the same level of achievement or in Billy's mind anyhow?

Is jealousy what we call somebody who's trying to bring us down to his or her lower level so they feel equal to us because they can't reach the same level of achievements? Billy feels obligated to do as well as Mike but can't so he tries to bring Mike down to his level so Billy's subconscious mind feels in balance. Is Billy a masochist and finds joy and pleasure in tormenting people? If Billy is a masochist he wouldn't be jealous of mike but sorry for him instead. A masochist finds pleasure in insults so maybe he thought he was doing Mike a favor by insulting him. If you can't understand why anybody would want to be a masochist how could you expect a masochist to understand why people don't want to be insulted? If Billy was a masochist it would explain why he has no friends. What was Billy's intention for insulting Mike?

The world is a very complicated place full of hidden truths. If Billy was a masochist he would want to be insulted because that bring him pleasure. So Billy might have thought that by insulting Mike he was bring him pleasure. Maybe Billy thought that Mike's girlfriend wasn't right for him and Billy was trying to break them up. Maybe by insulting Mike, Billy was subconsciously asking for help to achieve more. As a philosopher you can't just pick the first idea of why Billy was insulting Mike and label it as jealousy and then forget about it and move on to the next problem. To think as a philosopher you must consider all the possible angles that could come into play or you won't come to a logical solution.

In order to take a stand on an issue the philosopher must look at all possible angles. If you miss anything then you could be wrong in your philosophy on an issue. In the chapter on logic I'll go into this with more detail but if you miss an issue your logic will be wrong. So any time you're trying to establish a philosophy on something think of every angle you can. That goes double on philosophies of the mind.

Do you think your mind keeps your memories in a big filing cabinet? Any time you want to see an old memory your mind pulls it out of a filing cabinet and shows you the old memory. Take a second and answer that to yourself. If an old memory was nothing more than an old picture the picture will always look the same. The mind recreates the memory when you need it. After the memory is recreated you use your new philosophies to look the memory over. As you get older we adopt new philosophies and drop old views. That's how people mature. After you drop old philosophies and have new philosophies you apply your new philosophies to your old memories. That's one of the reasons you have a new outlook on life. It's also a great way to stop making the same mistakes. What's the definition of insanity? It's doing the same thing over and over again and expecting a different result.

When I was ten years old I had the philosophy of there is nothing better than baseball cards. I would mow people's yards for money to buy baseball cards and think I was slick for getting people to pay me worthless money so I could turn the worthless money into the most important thing in the world, which was baseball cards. Yes-sir-ree there was nothing better than baseball cards. I remember walking home from the store with a mouthful of bubble gum thumbing through my new baseball cards grinning like an idiot. That was my philosophy at ten years old and I can still picture it as vivid as the day it was happening. I'm now 38 years old and as you might have guessed my philosophy has changed. Baseball cards are no longer important to me and money is no longer worthless. When I was ten I collected baseball cards, that hasn't changed. I thought I was slick for getting people to pay me money so I could buy baseball cards, that hasn't changed. I remember walking home from the store chewing bubble gum and looking over my new cards, that hasn't changed. The only thing that has changed was my philosophy on collecting baseball cards. Today baseball cards are worthless and money is important to me now. Well money is one of the things important to me now.

How fast can a person's philosophy change? Let's say that two men are arguing. The one man decides to punch the other man in the face. So he balls his hand into a fist and pulls it back and swings hitting the other man in the face. While he's punching the other man his philosophy is it's important to punch this man in the face. If he didn't have that philosophy he wouldn't have done it. As the other man is falling to the floor the puncher might think to his or her self I shouldn't have punched the other man because there are other ways to settle an argument. A person's philosophies can change that fast.

In order to think like a philosopher it is so important to listen to all other philosophies with an opened mind so you can make the very best possible stand on a philosophy that you have. If you don't listen to all other premises or you miss some premises then you might have the wrong philosophy. If you refuse to listen or consider other views and you remain with your philosophy, that could be wrong, then you're condemned to making the same mistakes or to never find out the real truth of an issue. To be narrow-minded is to commit to the excepting of ignorance. If you wish to be ignorant of a new philosophy then you're trying to live in your own little reality. Adopting new philosophies and applying them to your old memories is by far the best way to not make the same mistakes over and over again. That's how to think like a philosopher.

So memories are from our past but can memories also go the other way and show or create images from the future? If memories, are only images from our past then what do we call images of the future that haven't happened yet? I'm sitting here writing a book and I can see images of people coming up to me saying, "Nice book Frank." I haven't even gotten the book published yet and I can see these make believe images as plain as day. If I can see images from the future how come I can't see the winning lottery numbers and not have to work anymore? Could it be our memory that makes up untrue pictures of the future but instead of acknowledging them to be from our memories we call it an active imagination? Is there a separate part of our mind that is our active imagination or is it our memories giving the illusion of things that might happen?

Another philosopher might argue that the active imagination, although very inspiring, is nothing more than daydreaming, which is still dreaming. It is impossible to see the future therefore we can only consider the active imagination to be daydreaming. I'm in Minnesota right now but I can see myself walking on a beach in some exotic land. If you can see yourself walking on a beach then it must be a dream because in reality you could not see yourself walking on a beach. If I'm holding a glass bottle in my hand I could use my active imagination to picture what the bottle would look like after I throw it down on a rock and break it. In my mind I can see broken pieces of glass that used to be a bottle but I haven't thrown the bottle yet but I can still picture the out come. If I do in fact throw the bottle against the rock it would break and my active imagination would have been right. If I do write a good book people will say, nice book Frank to me. So once again my active imagination is correct. Do you agree with this philosophy?

Another philosopher could argue that those actions are predetermined universal knowledge that most people already know. People know that if you throw a glass bottle on a rock hard enough it will in fact break. What the active imagination doesn't know for sure is how many pieces it will break into or what exactly those pieces will look like. Therefore nobody can see a true image of the future. People also know that if you write a good book you should get some compliments on the book that's universal knowledge. Therefore the active imagination is a great tool to inspire people to do things to get rewards or solve problems. If we had no active imagination what so ever than people wouldn't be able to solve problems because they couldn't have any possible idea of the out come of their actions. Therefore the active imagination is a great tool for inspiration and to help solve problems but it no way gives us images of the true future.

Yet another philosopher might say, we can learn from our mistakes if we had no active imagination. If we do something the wrong way and can see that the attempt didn't meet our needs we could try it a different way until we are successful. People can easily learn from their mistakes and only a fool would do the same thing over and over again. Therefore our active imagination is for our amusement only, the same way our dreams at night when we're sleeping, and really isn't necessary.

Our active imagination is in fact necessary because if we didn't have it and try to learn from our mistakes how would we know what we're trying to accomplish if we can't see what we're trying do? If we have no idea of what we want because we have no active imagination then how do we know we want something in the first place? If we have no active imagination and can't see make believe images of the future how do we know if we want something or how do we solve a problem? The active imagination is very much needed to see make believe images of what we believe to be the future.

Yet another philosopher might say, "It's the creative imagination that solves problems and not the active imagination." The active imagination is used to inspire you to do the actions you're thinking about doing but it's the creative imagination that actually solves the problem. Most people don't have any trouble using their active imagination but some do run into trouble using their creative imagination. Right now I'm writing a book using my creative imagination to help solve the problem of what to write to express my views to the reader. I'm using my active imagination to inspire me to continue doing so. What views do you have on the creative imagination? Do you share any of the views I talked about on the imagination? In order to think like a philosopher you must either agree or invent your own philosophies on the imagination.

Maybe all three are only one. Maybe the active, creative, and memories are only one imagination. Maybe we only have the illusion of having more than one. Do you think that's possible? If they're all separate imaginations then how many different non-physical entities are there in our brain? Let's see there is a memory, conscious mind, subconscious mind, active imagination, creative imagination, and our soul. I'm counting six different non-physical entities in one brain. Well that's quite a party going on in there. No wonder we have trouble making up our minds. Could all of these non-physical entities make up only one mind? A calculator has many different functions but only gives one correct answer. So can our minds have many different functions and give us one correct answer? If a calculator gives you a wrong answer then not all of the correct information was punched into the keypad. If a person comes up with the wrong answer then that person didn't perceive all the correct information as well. So a person could in fact come up with a wrong answer if they don't perceive or acknowledge all the information as being true or they're ignorant of some information as well.

So if a sperm cell can have a mind and an egg cell can have a mind a person could in fact have to separate minds in one brain. If the egg splits in two to form twins then both minds have to split as well so each twin has a conscious and subconscious mind. So it's possible to split a mind into two but if we have a conscious and a subconscious mind then it appears that we can't splice the minds together. So it's possible to split a mind but not to splice them together. If it's possible to split a mind and the mind will be equally split then is it safe to assume that our minds were split off of another mind. The mind you have now might have been split off from your parents. Your parent's mind might have been split off from their parent's mind as well and so on and so on until we get to where the first mind actually started. Is it possible that we all have a little piece of the original mind that started it all? That means that we are all sharing the same mind as one another. Is that why we are able to get along so well?

If were all sharing a little piece of the original mind then it would be safe to assume that we're sharing the same mind that Aristotle, Plato, and Pascal shared. Is that why we feel that there's a life after death because our mind some how knows that it's going to split again and go to our offspring? Could our children be our mind's life after death? If every time a woman gives birth to a child the mind is split so the child could also have a mind as well? Our children resemble the parents but what if the mind resembles the parents as well? If our physical body can reproduce than why can't our non-physical mind reproduce? If our minds were all split off from the original mind of thousands of years ago it would help explain instinct. A mind that's been around for thousands of years would have a good idea of how to survive and know what to do.

When a baby is born in the hospital the doctor who's delivering the baby doesn't give the baby crying lessons. The doctor doesn't tell the baby, "Okay, cry when you're hungry or you want to be picked up." Yet the baby automatically knows to do that. When a colt is born the mother horse doesn't start giving it standing lessons. Yet the baby colt stands up only minutes after it's born. So how do we have instincts? How do we automatically know what to do to survive? Instincts are non-taught biological capabilities. Do these instincts come from years of experience from the original mind?

Another philosopher might say, "It was God who gave us a mind at the first sign of life. Since it was God who created the mind God gave the mind some predetermined knowledge of what to do." Since it was God who gave us our mind it's also understandable that God wants us to be good so God gave us a subconscious mind as well to help guide us through determining right from wrong during our life. That's one of the reasons why we feel guilty then we do something wrong." Another might say, "God gave us our mind a long with the holy spirit, which is also a mind that we sometimes refer to as our subconscious mind to help guide us through life's challenges of knowing right from wrong." What do you think of these philosophies?

We can't really do anything without get instructions on how to do something. How does our mind know to keep the heart beating in a certain rhythm? Did God give us a predetermined knowledge of how to keep our hearts beating? Is it possible that our minds figure that out on it's own? Do babies that die of crib death simple forget to keep their hearts beating? Is our minds all split off of an original mind of thousands of years ago that already knows how to keep a heart beating and is just applying the knowledge that it already knows to help us survive? Is the mind that we refer to as our subconscious mind, really the Holy Spirit guiding us from wrong to right? These philosophies could apply to human beings but animals have instincts as well.

Animals have instincts just like people except animals have no right and wrong. Everything the animal does is to survive. So an animal doesn't really have a subconscious mind or does it? A philosopher might say, "Animals don't have life after death because they have no soul." What exactly is a soul? While where alive we refer to the soul as the mind and only after death does it in fact become a soul. Animals have minds of some sort. Yes, but animals do exactly what they need to do to survive therefore they never do anything wrong to answer to God about therefore they have no soul because they in fact don't have a subconscious mind or Holy Spirit. Another philosopher might say, "I own a dog. My dog knows that he's not aloud on my kitchen table because I punish him every time he jumps on the table. One time I came into the kitchen so quietly that I caught my dog on the table and he ran looking for cover to avoid the punishment he knew was coming. Therefore animals or at least dogs have a subconscious mind and do have feelings of guilt. If a dog can have feelings of guilt then the dog must have the Holy Spirit and then therefore must have a soul or life after death." Do you think dogs have a soul and go on after death?

Yet another philosopher might say, "Your dog has no subconscious mind and doesn't have any guilty feelings because your dog knew you would punish him for being on your table and ran for cover to avoid the punishment and not to show feelings of guilt. If your dog had the Holy Spirit and did have a sense of right and wrong he wouldn't have gotten on the table after you punished him the first time." Therefore we must assume that he knew he was going to be punished and ran because he knew what you would do and not because he felt guilty. Therefore your dog showed intelligence and not a subconscious feeling of guilt. An animal will do what ever they can to survive and if that means going behind your back to look for food on the table and getting punished if he gets caught then so be it. Your dog was following basic animal instincts looking for food and nothing else because dogs have no subconscious feelings of guilt but only of survival.

If that was the case then I don't do bank robberies because I don't want to get caught and sent to prison. I have a subconscious mind and don't do bank robberies and if I get caught and go to prison then so be it. Even though some people do exactly that. I know beyond the shadow of a doubt that bank robbery is wrong and if I get caught I'll go to prison. I also know that if I do a bank robbery and get away I'll benefit from the deed. So am I only showing intelligence, which is a basic animal instinct? Which means that I don't have the Holy Spirit or a subconscious mind to guide me? That could also mean I have no life after death? If my dog could get on the table and not get caught then he would benefit from the food he stole off the table. In either case both the dog and myself know right from wrong. So why wouldn't both of us have a subconscious mind?

In order to think like a philosopher we must look at all aspects of the human mind in order for us to make the best possible assumption on what we believe to be true. All of the arguments had good points in their own rights. We must consider all point or miss a premise and come to an illogical answer on our philosophies. These issues are too important to not make the right decision on. Take a minute and review and think of which one makes the most sense to you or invent your own philosophy on the issue.

A physicalist might say, "We have no subconscious mind but only a feeling of right and wrong from the way our society dictates to us what's right and what's wrong." Maybe the mind has no control of our heart beating. When we drink alcohol it impairs our ability to drive a car but does not impair our ability to keep our hearts beating. Alcohol is a physical thing. Our body is a physical thing. One physical thing can only impair another physical thing. Therefore our mind is a physical thing. When we drink alcohol it impairs our mind. Therefore our mind must be a physical thing. Our bodies can in fact die and our body is a physical thing. If our mind is a physical thing then it too in fact can die. If our mind was a non-physical entity then it wouldn't scrums to the effects of a physical thing such as alcohol. Therefore our minds are physical and we learn right and wrong by learning from society. We also have a subconscious feeling of guilt because we know that we did something wrong or against the rules of society. Therefore we do not have the Holy Spirit because the Holy Spirit, if it were true, would be a non-physical thing. A non-physical thing, if one existed, could not deal with a physical thing as our minds. Just because you can't picture what it would be like to be dead and no long exist doesn't mean that it's not true. Just because you can't see a micro-cell with the naked eye doesn't mean it doesn't exist. Therefore our minds are a physical thing.

A dualist might argue that yes it's true that alcohol is in fact a physical thing and does affect another physical thing, which is the brain not the mind. The mind is using a physical thing called the brain to move a physical thing such as a body. The brain, which is in fact a physical thing, being used by a non-physical thing called the mind so the physical body will do what the mind wishes it to do to serve the mind or soul. When you drink alcohol, which is a physical thing, it impairs the brain, which is a physical thing. Then the physical brain is impaired it makes it more difficult for the non-physical mind to communicate it's wishes to the brain to give the illusion that the mind is in fact impaired but it's the brain not the mind that's impaired by the alcohol. If the non-physical mind has trouble using the impaired brain then it's safe to assume that the Holy Spirit also must have trouble using the impaired brain as well. Since alcohol is in fact a physical form of a drug it makes the connection between the brain and the mind weaker, which gives the illusion to the mind of being soothed and comforted by the alcohol.

If I was bare foot and stepped on a nail and it punctured my foot my mind would find out about what has happened and tell my foot to get off the nail. If my body could think of an answer on it's own it would have no need to consult with the mind on what to do. If my body or foot could figure out what to do about the nail that punctured it then my mind would've never found out about the foot stepping on the nail because my foot already took care of the problem of what to do about the nail in it. The body has no way to figure out it's own solutions so all it can do is report everything to the mind through it's senses. When the body drinks alcohol it becomes impaired and all it can do is report to the mind through it's senses that it's in fact impaired which is the feeling of being soothed and comforted. Therefore the feeling you get from alcohol is nothing more than senses informing the mind that it's experiencing the effects of alcohol. What do you think about this philosophy? Is the feeling of alcohol nothing more than our senses?

People generally talk about physical items being cars, food, and the body as something you can feel and see. People talk about non-physical items as thinking, feeling, and dreaming as non-physical or mental entities. Entities are ontological units that exist in their own little world but not truly in the physical world. You can't see feel or touch a non-physical entity. So is fire an entity? Yes you can see fire and you can also feel fire but can you hold fire in your hand? How much does fire weigh? Fire breaths air and it consumes what ever it's burning. If you take away its fuel it will, to use the term, die out. If you take away its air supply it will die out. Do we kill an entity when we put out a fire? What is the definition of life? It's the quality of being alive. Fire eats what ever it burns and it breathes air. It is to some to be considered a non-physical entity.

If fire is a non-physical entity because it has no weigh than so must our minds be a non-physical entity that lives. Let's say that we can only see or feel fire when it gets to a certain temperature. After we cool the fire off we can no longer see or feel the fire and we consider the fire to be put out or gone. Is it possible for the fire to still exist if we can no longer see or feel it? Dog whistles can hit pitches so high that the human ear can't pick them up. So because we can't see, hear, or feel the whistle does that mean the high-pitched sound doesn't exist? Our senses can only report to our minds what they can actually pick up. So what if our senses are missing some of the things going on around us? If its possible to miss the high pitched sound of the whistle then it must be possible to miss other sounds or entities as well. What do you think about fire?

Electricity can be seen and felt but how much does it weigh? Electric impulses, is what the mind uses to move our body around. Electricity is what people use to run their appliances. We can see electric moving. We can feel the jolt it gives us when we touch it but where does it go when its no longer in our sight? Electric is a non-physical entity. Electric impulses is what our mind uses to move our bodies around so is electric similar to our mind? Does electric go on after we're done seeing it? Do you consider electric to be physical or non-physical? If so, why do you think that?

For years man has been searching for answers on the unknown world of life after death and what happens to us after we die. The unknowing is by far the scariest part of dying. People aren't scared of thinks that they know and understand. If you're religious and believe in God then you believe in life after death and have no problems thinking of your own death. If you're an atheist, and don't believe in God, then you must assume that you go back into the same existence you were in before you were born which is really nothing. Nothing isn't exactly painful so you too shouldn't worry much about death, if, however, you're correct in your philosophy. If an atheist is wrong in their philosophy then things aren't looking really good for the atheist.

I was told a story of a person that lived back in the 1600's was so curious about where we go after death that the person committed suicide to find out. I don't know if the story is true or not. I find it hard to believe anybody would in fact commit suicide to find out what happens after our mind or bodies die but I would not recommend doing what that person did. You'll find out soon enough without doing something as ill rational as committing suicide. Why would anybody consider suicide in the first place?

Suicide can only be committed by intelligent beings with the capability of reasoning things out. Animals don't commit suicide. They some times fail to think thing through but they never intentionally kill themselves. A mouse that gets his neck broke in a mousetrap had no intentions of getting killed he was only after the food that baited him to the trap. Since the mouse failed to reason out why some food was left out for him he stuck his head into the trap and SNAP had his neck broke by the trap. The mouse didn't wake up and say, "I had it with eating all these nasty leftovers and I'm going to stick my head into the trap and end my meaningless life once and for all." Mice don't know they can die. A deer in the woods will see a deer hunter on the other side of the field and just stand there looking at the hunter thinking, "I don't need to run away yet because I've got a really good head start and I can easily out run this deer hunter." What the deer fails to realize is that the hunter has a high-powered deer rifle and can easily shoot the deer from where he's at without even taking another step toward the deer. The deer doesn't understand how a rifle works so the deer just stands there thinking he has the advantage. The deer didn't think, "I'm tiered of living outside in these cold winters so I'll let the deer hunter shoot me and put me out of my misery."

I was watching on TV were they were giving a police dog trainer a dog's medal of bravery. The police dog ran in to attack an armed gunman. The gunman shot the dog but the dog still managed to down the gunman. Later the dog died of complications from the gunshot. That dog didn't know it could be killed. It knew it could be hurt but not killed. The dog also failed to realize that the gunman would shoot him also. I do find it incredible that the dog still got the gunman even after he got shot. This dog was truly incredible but didn't commit suicide and didn't know it could die. Don't get me wrong thank goodness for police dogs and their trainers.

Nobody really knows for sure who discovered the possibility that it's possible to take your own life. For all we know some caveman walked up and kicked a dinosaur and successfully committed the first suicide. Suicide is one of the top killers in the teenage years of human beings. What state of mind, does somebody have to be in to consider suicide? Does the mind know that it won't die and will go on living and still have an after life? Does the person feel hopeless? Is suicide just a snap decision to do because they're upset or is it planned out well in advanced? Somebody couldn't possibly use their active imagination in considering suicide because then they would have to picture the future result of them being dead. I wish I had the answer to this philosophical question.

An atheist that would consider suicide because they think that being dead is going back into the same existence you were in before you were born which is nothing but would deprive themselves out of everything that they had. A religious person who would consider suicide would think of how they intend to explain their actions to the almighty. I don't think God wants people committing suicide. Yet people do it all the time. Do these people lack reasoning? Was their situation so unbearable that they couldn't deal with it? People normally change when their present situation is so unbearable that change is inevitable. Do these people lack the creative mind need to solve the problem?

I had a cousin and his parents were getting a divorce. He told me, "Frank something's going to happen to bring my family back together." I said, "What did you figure out the winning lottery numbers?" I regret saying that because one week later my 23-year-old cousin committed suicide. He did the act in his car in front of the town's fire department. The police were the first to discover his body and suicide note. The family did get back together long enough to bury him but it only made the divorce more final. The mother was blaming the father and the father was blaming the mother he left a girlfriend behind who he was still in good standing with when he did the suicide. The parents were trying to say that he didn't know the gun was loaded and that the shooting was an accident. The insurance company didn't pay off because they have it down as a suicide. Every single person felt like it was some how their fault he committed suicide. I lost a lot of respect for my cousin for putting everybody through so much grief.

There is a tremendous amount of grief when a loved one commits suicide. Suicide is one of the most selfish thing anybody could possible do. Suicide is a lot different than sacrificing him or her self. If a soldier in a war jumps on a live grenade to save the lives of everybody else in the foxhole that soldier sacrificed him or her selves to save others. That's a whole different ball game. It wasn't a selfish thing that they've committed but an honorable deed. I don't understand suicide as well as I would like. I've only known two people that committed suicide. I'm not the leading expert on why people commit this hideous act of suicide, nor do I understand it full myself. What's your philosophy on suicide? Why do you think somebody would actually commit it? What kind of mind would commit suicide? I don't believe it to be the active imagination. Suicide is not my favorite subject but I try not to avoid it but often I find myself doing just that.

This concludes the human mind please feel-free to read it again if need be. In order to think like a philosopher it's important to look at all possible philosophies and views in order to make your best possible decision on where you stand on these issues. You wouldn't want to make a wrong decision on any of the views we talked about in this chapter. As you can see there is no set answers in philosophy only what you believe to be true. We base our beliefs on the most logical or rational answers we know or believe to be true. By looking at other views no matter how absurd they may sound at first and keeping an opened mind you're well on your way to thinking like a philosopher and will have one up on your competitor's for starting your own business or managing a preexisting small business. It's only the open-minded people who are capable of learning new things and getting all they can out of life. Narrow-minded people are usually condemned to live the same old mistakes over and over again. The definition of insanity is doing the same thing over and over again and expecting a different result.

Chapter Six

Business Reality

What is reality? Reality is what you believe to be real. Things can only be real if we believe they are in fact real. If you believe the Boogieman is a childhood make believe monster than he isn't real. If you were four years old you would believe in the Boogieman and he would be real. So to children the Boogieman is a reality. I remember when I believed in the Boogieman and I would protect myself by pulling up the covers. Everybody knows the Boogieman can't get you if you're under your covers. I would have a nightlight to ward off the derided Boogieman and other nighttime monsters that seemingly only attack children. Yes-sir-ree nice thick covers and a nightlight would protect you from a lot of nighttime monsters and especially the mean old Boogieman. Did you believe in the Boogieman when you were four years old?

In order to think like a philosopher you must use more than your senses to view the external world. Most people surprisingly take everything at face value while determining what reality is in the external world. The adverage individual believes that he or she can see with their eyes, however, unfortunately, this is not true. We see with our minds and not with our eyes. How accurately do our senses report to us what is really going on in the external world? A Magician can deceive your eyes and get you to believe they're pulling a rabbit out of a hat or sawing a woman into two pieces and then put her back together again. Magicians make a living off of deceiving your eyes and performing illusions that people call magic. If we are to assume the magician is real then we are only going by what our eyes tell us with no though to what is really going on. If we see a magician performing tricks and know it's only an illusion then it's safe to assume that we know our sense of sight is being deceived. If a magician can deceive our eyes then it therefore means that other illusions can deceive our eyes as well. How accurately do your eyes serve you? Do you think your eyes could be wrong at times? Do you believe everything you see to be real?

The first group of reality I refer to is the primal group. People in the primal group view the external world the same way that animals do. They take everything at face value and don't doubt their senses at all. If a person in the primal group can put their hands on it or see it they consider it to be real and don't give it a second thought. Can you see anything wrong with that? If I would take a very large mirror and put it out in the middle of the jungle what do you think would happen? If a lion would come walking by and see it's self in the mirror the lion would take it at face value and snarl at it's own image in the mirror which would then appear to be snarling back at the lion. I think the lion would break the mirror thinking it was attacking another lion to defend its territory. Yes, I think something from the primal group would have come along and broke the mirror. I mean how many mint condition mirrors do you see in the jungle?

One of the knights from king Arthur's round table would on certain occasions walk over to a lake and draw his sword to dip the blade into the water. Then when he looked at the sword it gave the illusion of being bent where it went into the water. The knight knew his sword wasn't bent but he did it as a reminder that it's possible to misinterpret the external world. This knight belonged to the logical group of people who apply what they know of the world to what they see, feel, hear, and smell. People in the logical group can understand that it's possible to misinterpret the external world. Philosophers belong to the logical group also known as causal realism not to be confused with common-sense realism.

Commonsense realism; is viewed by everybody who hasn't studied philosophy. It's the most basic of ways to monitor the external world. It lets everybody assume that there is a world out there that's filled with lots of physical object like sports cars, new houses, other people, money, and Olivofonics: Small Business Management & Philosophy books. We can learn everything we need to know through our five senses and these physical objects continue to exist whether we're perceiving the object or not. They assume that the objects they're seeing are exactly as they appear to be. Grasshoppers are green, the ocean is flat and blue, and money can buy everything. Our senses of sight, sound, feel, smell, and taste are generally reliable and give us a realistic perception of what's going on in the external world around us. I can see and understand how it's possible to go around all of your life with this philosophy. However I wouldn't recommend it.

Rene Descartes (1596-1650) wrote the Cogito ergo sum: I think therefore I am. Descartes philosophy was to locate the point of certainty in your own awareness of your own self. In other words knowledge starts with the quest for certainty, for indubitable starting point or foundation on the basis alone of which progress is possible. In order to be understood by others, we must first seek to understand. We can never know anything for certain that there is always some doubt even to our most fundamental beliefs about the external world around us. Our fundamental ways of finding out about the world are unreliable and don't guarantee us knowledge of what truly exists in the external world around us. There are some uncontroversial instances of knowing through which we learn the concept of knowledge and it's only because we have these backgrounds of instances of knowledge that we can doubt other beliefs. If we didn't have other previous instances that we could compare to, we would have no concept of knowledge at all. If we have no previous instances to compare things to we would in fact have nothing with which to contrast more doubtful beliefs. How do you understand the external world?

In order to think like a philosopher you must understand the basic principal of where your mind is and how it interprets the external world around us. What do I mean by where your mind is and external world? Our mind is enclosed inside our brain, which is enclosed in a skull. Our mind finds out what's going on in the external world by the use of organs, such as our eyes, ears, nerve endings, nose, and taste. These organs can be fooled into believing the wrong thing about the external world around us. For example, a bird flying into a plate glass window, the bird had no prior instances of glass and took his sight at face value and flew right into the window. People some times walk into windows too but at least they knew what happened. If you close your eyes your mind is no longer seeing what's going on in the external world. Therefore you can understand what it's like to be blind. A bird wouldn't close its eyes to see what it would be like to be blind therefore birds use commonsense realism to make their way in the external world.

Let's say you're in a car with no windows at all. There's a TV camera mounted on the hood of the car and it's sending images to a monitor that's mounted right in front of you where you would normally look when driving your car. The only knowledge of what's going on in the world in front of the car is being projected to you on the monitor that's in front of you. How fast would you drive the car? If you believe the images to be true you would drive the speed limit. If you didn't believe the images you would drive very slow or not at all. How fast would you drive if I gave you two cameras? Every time you drive your car you're doing exactly that, going by the two cameras mounted above your nose called eyes. When driving conditions are foggy you slow down and when driving conditions are sunny you drive the speed limit going by the images that your eyes are giving to your mind and that my friend is the real reality.

Then there is the possibility of hallucination. Hallucinations are different than dreams. It's possible to know we're dreaming because dreams have a different effect than reality. In dreams everything is hazy or its not the same quality as when we're awake plus you can't ask yourself. "Am I dreaming in a dream?" Hallucinations however can occur when we're wide-awake and when we know we're wide-awake. So hallucinations are a reality but how is that so?

Even if I'm not dreaming, I may be hallucinating. Some madman might have slipped some LSD or some other mind-altering drug into my cognac while I was at the club. Even though I know I'm awake, maybe I don't have a pen in my hand writing a book. Maybe I'm not sitting in my den writing a book and listening to soft music. Maybe I've reached such a high state of alcoholism that I'm starting to hallucinate. If the chair, which I'm sitting in, is only imaginary then how does it support my weight? Maybe I'm hallucinating to the fact that I'm sitting down in the first place. I might think I'm sitting in a comfortable chair but in reality I'm sitting on a box. Maybe I shouldn't have drunk the whole bottle of cognac in one sitting. No you're not reading a book that was written by an alcoholic, even though I enjoy cognac tremendously I'm incapable of drinking a whole bottle in one sitting or well currently I'm incapable of doing that.

When a person is using the commonsense realism philosophy to make their way in the external world it's possible to hallucinate on what reality is. Somebody driving in traffic might see all the other cars cutting them off and think that everybody is out to get them. This develops into paranoia. A paranoid person is hallucinating to what they believe to be true. The world is neither good nor evil but only in how you perceive it to be. Do the other drivers in traffic cut you off for the sole purpose of upsetting you or because they don't want to miss their turn and weren't smart enough to get into the right lane to make their exit? I find it hard to believe that a driver following you would think, "Hum, my exits coming up. I think I'll speed up and cut the car off in front of me while I'm taking my exit. This way I can upset the driver in front of me and still take my exit at the same time." How absurd to believe another driver is thinking that. The driver that cut you off is either selfish or ignorant to the ethics of driving a car. If you do believe that other drivers are out to get you then that's exactly what you believe they're thinking.

People who practice commonsense realism are so quick to put labels on other people that they fail to notice a person's full potential. By quickly labeling other people the commonsense realism philosophy user no longer has to think about the other person and can go on with other important things like watching TV. Let's do an example. Let's say you're on a parole board committee and are going to review an inmate who is eligible for parole from prison.

Parole board: Why do you think we should grant you parole? Inmate: I didn't do the crime that I'm accused of doing and you should let me go because I'm really innocent. PB: Did you give a confession when they arrested you? IMT: Well I gave more of a statement and then retracted it one hour later. PB: Did you plead guilty to the charge? IMT: I pleaded guilty to a lesser charge because my lawyer said they had enough evidence to convict me if I plead not guilty. So I took the lesser of the two evils and plead guilty to the lesser charge. PB: If you were innocent why would you plead guilty to anything? IMT: I'm more or less a victim of circumstances. The evidence they had made me look really guilty but none of it was really hardcore and for sure so I took the plea bargain. PB: Did you plead guilty because you are in fact guilty and you didn't want to chance getting more time? So you took the lesser charge, which gave you less time so you could get out of the real time a crime like that demands. IMT: No, No it's nothing like that I really didn't do the crime they're accusing me of doing. PB: We've decided to decline your parole, but will review it again next time you're eligible for parole. I'm here to tell you sir we are not stupid. You took the plea bargain because you're in fact guilty. You should be grateful to receive less time than what you had coming. Anybody who can't acknowledge that they've done something wrong isn't ready to be paroled. IMT: No you got it wrong weren't you listening to me? I didn't do it. I'm a victim of circumstances that's all. I didn't break the law ever.

Do you agree with the parole boards findings? Is the inmate guilty as charged? Is the inmate just trying to pull a fast one so he could get paroled? If you agreed with the parole board then you're guilty of using the commonsense realism philosophy. A philosopher would have said, "We're going to reschedule your parole hearing for two weeks from today so we could look at the court records and get to the bottom of this. In order to think like a philosopher you must realize that we live in a very complicated world. You can't just label things as best you see them in five minutes and then forget about it. As a philosopher you must look at all the angles to base your decisions on. People have in fact given up one of their kidneys to a loved one who needed a kidney to live. So why wouldn't a person confess to a crime and take the punishment so a love one who did the crime wouldn't have to go to prison? Is it possible that the inmate didn't know his rights well enough that he pleaded guilty because everybody kept telling him it's the smartest thing to do? Maybe the inmate knew that people on the jury would be using the commonsense realism philosophy and the evidence looked so convincing that they would've convicted him. The only information you have on this inmate is what I've told you. Is that enough information for you to make a decision on a man's life? If after two weeks you find he was in fact guilty you could then turn him down on parole.

The world is truly a complicated place and can't be summed up in five minutes. Con-artists look for people who act before they think. This way they can get the money and run. Reality is what you believe to be true. Things that we believe to be true, is our knowledge. If a con-artist can get you believe their scam then it becomes reality to you and you won't hesitate to give them your money. Labeling things as fast as you can is another way of saying I don't want to think about it. With this philosophy you're going to miss out on a lot of good stuff.

Causal realism is the philosophy that I use to make my way around the external world. Causal realism assumes that the causes of our sense experience are in fact physical objects in the external world. Causal realism takes as its starting point the observation that the main function of our senses is to help us find our way in the external world. It is through our senses that we acquire knowledge about the external world around us. Causal realism allows us to use our senses as a starting point or foundation on which to build our beliefs on the external world but still allows us to realize that our senses could in fact be wrong. According to the causal realism's philosophy, when I see my car what actually happens is that light rays bouncing off my car cause certain affects on my retinas and other areas of my brain, this leads me acquiring certain beliefs about what I'm seeing. The experience of acquiring the beliefs is the experience of seeing my car. Does this philosophy sound logical to you?

The way by which we acquire our beliefs is very important, not just any old way will do. For me to actually see my car it is essential that my car is the cause of the beliefs I acquire about it. The appropriate causal link for seeing is that brought about by an object bouncing light rays on to my retinas and the processing of the information into my brain. If I was under the influence of drugs, for example, and was merely hallucinating, then this wouldn't be the case in seeing my car. The drug rather than the car would've been the cause of my beliefs.

Another great advantage of causal realism is that it can easily explain the fact our existing knowledge affects what we perceive. In acquiring information our system of classification, and our existing knowledge, directly affect how we treat incoming information and what we select and interpret as relevant or what is not worth thinking about. This is a great philosophical way to interpret the external world around us. Causal realism's metaphysical assumption is there is a real world out there that does exist independently from people perceiving it. In other words it is an assumption about the nature of reality. Life is but a dream? Is there an external world?

George Berkley (1685-1753) Said, "To exist is to be perceived." Berkley was an idealist and probably the most famous idealist in philosophy. Idealism is basically the denial of the reality of any external world. It argues that there is no justification for saying the external world exists at all. In idealism, things only exist if you are perceiving it at that moment. As soon as you can no longer perceive the thing you were looking at, it no longer exists. So if I go inside my house and no longer see my car it doesn't exist any more. I guess I better look out the window and make it reappear again because I'm going to need it tomorrow. According to idealism if I walk out of a room that room no longer exists because I no longer perceiving it. This whole idealism philosophy is absurd. Talk about being paranoid, if a tree fall in the woods and nobody's there to hear it fall does it still make a sound? You betcha! Idealism is for people who think the external world doesn't really exist and it's just a world full of minds thinking that there is some kind of external world and it's nothing more than a movie we're all watching. I think I'll pass on this philosophy and stick with causal realism.

We perceive the world through conceptual and linguistic lenses of our own making. If we misinterpret something and don't realize it we base our assumptions on the misinterpretation. Verbal communication is by far the easiest to misinterpret. People from different parts of the USA all talk with different accents and have different phrases to mean different things. Wars have started with verbal misinterpretations. People from the south say you-all and people from New York say you-guys and so on. We generally take one on one personal communications very seriously. We make direct eye contact with the person we're talking to and watch their movements as we're talking to them. The only problem is that verbal communication moves at a high rate of speed making it easier to misinterpret the speaker. Once a misinterpretation happens it's harder to straighten it out. It's important to pay attention to the speaker to avoid these misinterpretations. I was talking to a guy and asked him if he liked his jeep. He said, "Yes." but he was shaking his head no. So I said, "It's not what you wanted huh?" He said, "Oh I like my new jeep." Once again shaking his head no as he's saying yes. It takes that guy an hour and a half to watch sixty minutes on TV. That will teach me to trespass in his world of reality.

I was watching a movie with my girlfriend and her little girl, who was I think six years old at the time. We were watching an old war movie and the actor who was portraying an Englishman said, "I can't wait to get back to bloody old England." My girlfriend's little girl turned around to face us and asked, "Is it really bloody in England mommy?" In her little mind she though that England had blood splat-tered all over the buildings, the trees, and all over the place. She never heard that phrase before and misinterpreted it to be something else. What the actor really was trying to say was, "I can't wait to get back to good old England." Since verbal communication moves at such a fast pace she only got one shot at understanding what the actor was trying to say. Therefore she had to use her preexisting knowledge of what blood is and try and piece it together for herself. Bloody means more blood was her interpretation.

Written communication is easier to understand and harder to mis-interpret. If you don't understand something you just simply reread the parts you don't understand or look in the glossary. I've never met you and have no reason to insult you. You've never met me and you're paying me to help you think like a philosopher and start your own business, so you know I don't know you and have no reason what so ever to insult you. Therefore if you don't fully understand something you realize that you didn't fully understood what I was talking about and reread what you had trouble with. Oh yeah did I mention how grateful I am that you purchased my book? Thank you very much and I think you're a very intelligent person for doing so. I am truly pleased to meet you. How did you interpret what I just said? Did you take it as a feeble attempt at humor or did you think I was insulting you? Did you laugh or snarl when you read that? Now if somebody writes a personal letter addressed to a certain individual then it's possible that the writer is trying to insult the reader. As far as books go the reader has full control over the interpretation part of their reading. If it takes you a day to read this book so be it. If it takes a week so be it. You the reader can take your time and read this book till you fully understood what I was trying to tell you. On verbal communication it's a whole different story. Bloody right you are mate.

The world is neither an evil nor a good place but it's all in how you perceive it. Causal realism allows the philosopher to apply preexisting knowledge along with the senses to make the best possible decision on what reality is. This is by far the best way to think like a philosopher.

The world itself is very complicated and has many hidden dangers. That's why it's so pointless to make up some weird and paranoid assumptions about people or the world in general and add more dangers to your reality. It's even possible to misinterpret causal realism's philosophy as well. So if causal realism can in fact be misinterpreted then why am I recommending it? Well never under estimate the mind in reality. What happens when you use preexisting knowledge to interpret the external world around you?

Adolf Hitler used his preexisting knowledge of the hand full of Jews that he met to determine what to do with millions of Jewish people in the Holocaust. In the depression that followed the great depression of the 1920's Hitler saw a few Jewish people trying to survive the depression by holding onto their money. That's understandable they were just trying to survive the depression, I would've done the same thing. Hitler accused the Jews of hoarding their money. They were just trying to make sure that their family would survive the depression. In Hitler's sick little mind the Jews should've spent their money freely and it would've helped solve the depression. Well after Hitler became the chancellor of Germany in world war two he took his preexisting knowledge that Jews were money hoarders and applied it to all the Jews and killed millions in the Holocaust. Hitler didn't meet each and every Jew and based his opinion on the individual. Hitler built killing factories and killed millions of Jews during the Holocaust. So yes it's still possible to misinterpret even causal realism philosophy. It's also possible to misinterpret your preexisting knowledge as well.

In order to think like a philosopher you can't allow yourself to fall into the entire make believe realities of the external world. I've seen high society type people snub their nose at people who they believe don't make a lot of money. I had a woman in New York look me right in my eyes and tell me if I don't make $100,000.00, a year then we wouldn't have anything in common. She was very young at the time I hope her views have changed since then. There is nothing wrong with building your dream reality so you can live the life you want to but don't make the mistake of dreaming your reality. I've read motorcycle magazines that said a biker died and went to motorcycle heaven. Is there a motorcycle heaven? When George Washington finally died did God give him a new motorcycle? George might have said, "What in the world is this thing and what do I feed it?" If we're going to think like this, then when I die I go to philosopher's heaven and finally get all the correct answers to my philosophies? Yet motorcycle heaven is a reality to some bikers. Don't dream your life away. Dreaming up your own reality is a nice way to give yourself a false sense of security but it's not the answer for getting ahead in this world.

The world is neither an evil nor good place but it's all in how you perceive it to be. I can't stress that point enough. I meet so many people who are living in their own little reality that it sickens me to see it. Nothing is more upsetting to me than seeing my loved ones mindlessly living in their own reality of what they believe to be true. Working 30 years at a job they hate to do because they can't see any other possibilities or staying with an abusive spouse because an I quote "You know the devil your with." You can't do it friends it's not going to work. People are scared of changes. Changing is no doubt stressful but the definition of insanity is doing the same thing over and over again and expecting a different result. People normally change when their present situation is so unbearable or they're so miserable that change takes place because they can no longer stand the present situation another day. When their present situation gets to the point of they're contemplating suicide that's when they finally consider changing. When a person would rather live under a bridge then spend one more day with their abusive spouse they finally decide to change. So why does it always have to get to that point before people are willing to change? How do we get into these situations in the first place?

Let me give you a true-life story, of why I think people make up his or her own make believe realities. There was a woman married to an abusive husband. One day the woman had accidentally burned some steaks on the outdoor grill. They were in fact burned really bad and couldn't be eaten. The husband slapped her in the face and said, "See what you made me do? If you had half a brain I wouldn't have to knock some sense into you. Steaks cost money, stop wasting my hard earned money. Now what are we suppose to eat?"

The woman had the preexisting knowledge of you never slap somebody who accidentally burned a few steaks. If she would decide to leave she, she would also have the preexisting knowledge of, it would be very stressful to pack up all of her things and children and move out. Plus I don't have a career that could support my self and the children. So maybe if I don't burn anymore of the steaks he won't hit me again. It's much easier to change realities than it is to go through all the stress of moving and trying to live on what ever she could make for a living. Now the woman is living in her abusive husband's reality of slapping people who burn steaks is okay. If this was a real reality, then if a woman was living alone and she burnt some steaks what does she do?

Does she call the police department and say, "Hello, could you please send a policeman over to my house?" Then after the policeman shows up and she invites him in she says, "I burned some steaks on the grill by accident officer." The policeman looks at the burnt steaks and says, "Well I hate to do this lady but you know what reality is. Could you please keep your hands by your side and lean forward a little with your chin up so I can slap you for burning the steaks." Slap! "All this could've been avoided lady if you had half a brain I wouldn't have to drive over here and waste taxpayer's money to knock some sense into you. I don't enjoy slapping people and I'm upset that you made me do this to you. Next time you cook steaks be a little more careful." This is the absurd reality the woman was living in.

There is no doubt that it's easier to change realities than to change things in real life. In order to think like a philosopher you can't ignore preexisting knowledge and paint a new picture of what reality should be. The world is very complicated and there are no short cuts no matter how much you want them to be true. Philosophers live in reality by using their preexisting knowledge and not by creating make believe realities to over ride the fact that they have to change his or her life to solve a problem.   Philosophers aren't happy just living in a make believe world full of myths. To think like a philosopher you must acknowledge what reality is even if it's not a pretty picture. Life isn't easy and it's full of hidden dangers. Failure to see things the way they truly are is one of the biggest mistakes a person could make. Yet, millions of people choose to live life in their own little reality until things get so unbearable that change is unavoidable. Does it always have to get to that point of somebody contemplating suicide? Wouldn't it be smarter to acknowledge your preexisting knowledge of what reality is instead of suppressing what you do already know? By making up your own little reality people have to think less about what to do, which leaves more time for the really important stuff like watching TV. Why is solving problems something most people want to try and ignore? Is thinking such a hard chore that people would rather make up a reality than to think of a solution? You're responsible for your mind and your actions only and nobody else's. It's impossible for one person to change another person's mind. All a philosopher can do is layout what they believe to be true and hope others will agree with it. Now that's reality. I know because I've tried to change people's views and have failed to do so.

Well that concludes chapter six on business reality. Reality is what you believe to be true. Things that we believe to be true we consider to be our knowledge. So to the best of my knowledge reality is what you believe it to be. I recommend the causal realism philosophy over the commonsense realism philosophy because some times your senses can in fact be wrong. I know this because I have a preexisting knowledge that I apply along with my senses to make my way around the external world.

It is better for an abused woman to eat peanut butter and jelly sandwiches every day for two weeks than for her to allow her abusive husband to slap her. If she has to work two full time jobs to support her self than so be it. She'll have one thing that her abusive husband won't have. She'll be living in the real reality and not in some make believe land. Her husband will be condemned to live in his own little reality and suffer the consequences of repeating the same things over and over again expecting a different result and if the wife keeps living in the same reality as her husband then she is condemned as well. I just hope her X-husband doesn't work for the police department.

Another business related myth is that if customer service doesn't solve the problem, then it was poor customer service. This is not true. An employee can give great customer service even if the employee doesn't solve the problem. Give the best service you can, doesn't mean that you'll solve all the problems. As individuals, we all have limitations. If a customer things that because the problem wasn't solved, they received poor customer service, you don't need that individual as a customer. You cannot please everybody; I have a preexisting knowledge of this because at one time in my life, I did in fact try to please everybody. I don't believe it can be done.

Chapter Seven

Business Ethics

Ethics is different than etiquette. Etiquette is nothing more than being equal to what is required or a fully sufficient way of performing a certain ritual in a manner that is commonly acceptable or norms of a polite society. In other words a person who's slurping their soup in a restaurant may not be performing proper etiquette but may still have ethics and morals. People who practice etiquette are normally more disciplined and have perfected the philosophies of ethics and morals. However, people who have etiquette, or think they do, and look down on people who don't could in fact have no ethics or be ignorant to the fact that everybody practices ethics in a certain way. By doing this not only does a person have to have ethics but they must also perform his or her ethics in a certain way, which is acceptable to the beliefs of somebody who is practicing etiquette. Etiquette is a great way to discipline yourself in performing rituals in a manner that is commonly acceptable but it shouldn't be away of judging one person's etiquette against another person's morals or ethics. Etiquette and morals or ethics are in fact two different things. People who do practice etiquette do seemingly get invited out to dinner more often.

In this chapter we're going to look at the nitty gritty of ethics and morals and skip over etiquette all together in the hopes of making an ethically acceptable small business. In order to think like a philosopher, we're going to look at the conceptual questions of ethics, and how do we determine right from wrong and why we do. We're going to look at some of the philosophies of philosophers who have tried to answer some of the questions on why we perform ethics and why we do in fact have morals. Some of the philosophies might try and tell us why certain things are immoral and why we should have guidelines in the way we act. Some will question why a certain act is or isn't morally correct. Philosophy on ethics is divided into two basic parts. The first is duty based or deontological and the second is consequentialist philosophies on ethics.

Let's say we have a rich man who has a high paying job and he owns a new house, a new car, and has no trouble feeding himself. This man enjoys duck hunting for sportsmanship purposes only. On a hunting trip with his friends he sees a duck floating or swimming in the water. He turns to his friend and asks, "Is it legal to shoot the duck in the water?" Then it's safe to assume that this man is ignorant to what the ethics of sportsmanship are. By him asking if it's legal to shoot the duck in the water then he's really saying is, "I have no understanding of sportsmanship ethics. What are the rules saying about sportsmanship?" This man is using the deontological or duty based philosophy of ethics. Duty based ethics are rules that are established by people who do in fact understand the ethics of sportsmanship. If you're ignorant to an ethic then you simply follow the already established rules of ethics. It's your duty to follow the rules in order to have sportsmanship ethics.

Let's say we have another man who is dirt poor and only owns the clothes on his back. This man is starving and must eat in order to survive. The only weapon he has is a club that he made out of a piece of wood he found in the forest. This man too sees a duck sitting in the water. What should this man do? He should hit that duck in the head and eat it. Sportsmanship no longer applies here. It would be ludicrous to give that duck any chance what so ever to get away. The man's intentions were to feed him self and not to have fun shooting ducks. Intentions are the founding bases of consequentialist's philosophies on ethics. Yes he broke a rule of sportsmanship but he needed the duck to survive, so that was his intentions, which is the morally correct thing to do. So even though this man broke a rule he still had more ethics than the man who was hunting for sportsmanship, under the consequentialist's philosophy of ethics. A lion wakes up in the jungle and knows he must out run the slowest gazelle or suffer the consequence of starving to death. A gazelle wakes up in the jungle and knows he must out run the fastest lion or suffer the consequence of being eaten alive. It doesn't matter if you're a lion or a gazelle when you wake up you better be running.

Ethics is the study of problems of right and wrong conduct in the light of moral principals like compassion, justice, good, freedom and rationality. The word ethics itself comes from the Greek word "Ethos" it means character. Choices concerning what ethics to hold, how to treat yourself and your responsibilities to others is a matter of character, or values. Morality is derived from the Latin word "Mores" meaning customs. Etiquette and some times adequate are often confused with morals and morality is often confused with ethics. So was the rich duck hunter ignorant to the customs or morals of sportsmanship or was he confused with the proper etiquette of duck hunting? In order to think like a philosopher, we must sometimes make a distinction between ethics and morality. Holding ethics to refer to cultivation of our character and practical decision making, while morality or customs refers more generally to the set of guide lines society holds to be right or the proper adequate or etiquette to an action. So was the poor duck hunter ethical by practicing practical decision making in his quest for survival or was he ignorant to the adequate or etiquette of duck hunting?

Our ethical beliefs help us determine right from wrong. They help us to define good and bad and to try and realize our vision of the good in our actions. Ethical beliefs help us sort through differences of opinions over what is good and what is bad. "Why, is this the right thing to do?" and "What, is the right thing to do?" are the basis for ethical inquires. Some philosophers believe that it's a natural capability, like our ability to reason things out and others believe that our sense of right and wrong comes from God. Others believe that our knowledge of right and wrong comes from our experience from the external world around us. Which is it?

Christian moral teaching has dominated western understanding of ethics. Our whole basic conception of what ethics and morality is has been shaped by religious beliefs, and even atheist's ethical philosophies have adopted it. The Ten Commandments lists certain duties and forbidden activities. These duties apply regardless of the consequences of carrying them out. Those are absolute duties that are not negotiable. Anybody who believes in God has no trouble knowing right from wrong. Right is God's will and wrong is against God's will. In order for a Christian to have ethics all they have to do is God's will or follow the absolute duties. So killing is a sin. It's listed in the Ten Commandments and there's no way to misunderstand what it says. Thou shall not kill. Is there anyway to misunderstand that Commandment? So killing a certain individual, say Hitler, that could save millions of lives, is still a sin. What do you think? Would it have been a sin to kill Hitler and save millions of Jewish lives in or from the Holocaust? To kill Hitler would be against God's will even though it would've saved millions of lives.

What exactly is God's will? Ask any Christian and they'll point to the bible and say, "It's all in there." The bible is a physical thing and physical things can be misinterpreted. The bible wasn't originally written in English so it had to be translated at least once. How do we know that the translator knew what they were doing? Look at the book of Genesis, for example, some people think the world was literally created in seven days and some think it's only a metaphor. Did the translator mean it as a metaphor? Did they misinterpret it from the beginning? Some Christians believe it's acceptable to kill in times of war and some think that the Commandment thou shall not kill is absolute and unconditional. So which is it literally or metaphor, acceptable or unconditional? God's will is the way to morality but exactly what is God's will? Is it just the Ten Commandments?

To practice Christian ethics and morality is far more complicated than just simply following the Ten Commandments. If it was that easy you could just learn the Ten Commandments in one visit to church and never have to go back, how long does it take to learn Ten Commandments? Christianity involves the learning of Christ's teachings in the New Testament. It could in fact take a lifetime to learn to quote the bible. The basis of this philosophy of ethics and morality is a system of dos and don'ts, which is true on most other moralities based on religion. Christian ethics is a duty-based philosophy of ethics. God's will is right and against God's will is wrong. So to have ethics you simply do God's will to the best that you believe God's will to be.

Plato (427-347 BC) student of Socrates and teach to Aristotle. Plato wrote the "Euthyphro" Does God command or love what he or she does because it is morally good? Or does God's commanding or loving something make it morally good? If God commands or loves what he or she does because it's morally good then this makes morality independent of God. God is responding to preexisting moral values that were already there to begin with. Discovering morality rather than creating morality. On this philosophy it would be possible to describe morality without any mention of God. Even though it might be through God that provides us with a more reliable information about ethics than what we would otherwise be able to figure out with our mortal intelligence. If God creates right and wrong simply by his or her commanding or approving it to be, so then this seems to make morality somewhat one sided. In theory, God could have declared murder to be morally praiseworthy and it would have been so. A Christian would jump up and say how absurd for you to even think that, God would never make murder praiseworthy because God is good and would never condemn us to that morality. If by saying "Good" is meant "Morally Good" this has the meaning that all that "God is Good" can mean is "God approves of him or her" for following what God believes to be good. Nevertheless I don't think that's what Christians meant by saying God is good.

Plato is known for his idealism philosophy that ideas have a reality of their own or that they exist and have a feature of being independent of the physical world. Plato's philosophy is the things that we observe in our sense experiences are what they appear to be because they have certain characteristic forms expressed from our ideas. This philosophy is known as Plato's idea of form. For example Squares are squares because they have the form of squaralarity, which we understand that idea in our mind. Squares in the physical world are thought to be copies of our ideas or forms and even poor copies at best because nothing in the external world could ever be as perfect as the idea of squaralarity that's in our mind. In other words no square is a perfect square because we know what a perfect square would be like, do to our idea or definition of squaralarity that's in our mind. That's one of the reasons why Plato held artists at the bottom of the totem pole and philosophers at the top. Artists were copying the imperfect external world, which in a sense made his or her artwork even more imperfect than the original world's. It was okay to decorate a cup or plate to make it more attractive but just don't get carried away with it.

Plato's philosophy was also idealistic as well because the ideas such as virtue and justice express the kinds of perfection people would want to seek based on the ideas of justice that where in their minds. People do in fact have an idea of what justice should be. The punishment should fit the crime perfectly. Neither too harsh, nor too lenient. If a person kills another person what should his or her punishment be? The loved ones of the murder victim will say, "Off with that person's head." The family of the murder would say, "Have mercy, our family member truly didn't mean to commit murder and is still a human being. Two wrongs don't make a right. We don't think our family member should be put to death because he or she can still help mankind." Now we clearly have two separate ideas of what justice should be.

In the USA we simply send criminals to prison. That's our idea of justice. So if we have two men who commit the same crime they should get the same amount of time, right? Doesn't that sound fair to you? Let's say one of the men is suffering from claustrophobia? He couldn't stand to be in tight little rooms. Even though I've never been to prison I know the prison's cells aren't spacious and roomy. The man suffering from claustrophobia would be doing harder time than the other man who doesn't suffer from claustrophobia, isn't that right? Does that still sound fair to you? We could say, "He should've thought about that before he committed the crime in the first place." Ah there that feels better, we now shifted the problem off our shoulders and put the problem back on the criminal and made yet another misconception of what justice is in an imperfect world. So could Plato be right in saying we have a good idea of what things should be but have trouble applying them to the external world? If a person were willing to break a law then surely that person would be willing to lie? A criminal could lie about being claustrophobic in the first place. Then we would give them a bigger room and the person does easier time than somebody in a smaller room, is that right or fair to do? That wouldn't be justice but a misinterpretation of justice in an imperfect world.

That's not even considering a masochist or a sadist. A masochist and a sadist enjoy being insulted and tortured. So if a masochist or a sadist breaks a law, what do we do to punish them? Do we sentence them to live with the Brady Bunch? I can picture the masochist or sadist saying, "No not that your honor, anything but that. Greg and Marsha will treat me with respect and won't take offended by my insults. Please send me to prison your honor, anything but the Brady Bunch. Please show mercy." It would be a living hell for a masochist or a sadist to live with the Brady Bunch. Yes indeed it's quit a circus going on in the external world that we proudly call reality. What is perfect justice in an imperfect world?

According to Plato in order to be clear about such ideas, by philosophically examining, is to understand the goal of human life. One does in fact need to know or understand the idea of justice. In order to know what it means to be just is to aim for and achieve justice in one's life. Confusion about such ideas leads us in to errors of what justice may in fact be but the highest and most honorable of all ideas is the idea of the good in justice. Nevertheless, everything that's good is good because it participates in or has the characteristics of what good is being expressed by our idea of what goodness is. To aim at being virtuous or just is nevertheless to aim at being good, which is the goal of the virtuous or moral life. So if we could in fact produce our ideas perfectly in the external world we would in fact have justice in the world. Until that time comes is it ethically or morally correct to use only guidelines to administer justice? To the best of my knowledge we've never achieved perfect justice in the external world. That alone could be considered a crime in it's self.

According to Plato the existence of ideas doesn't depend on our thinking about them or on how we define them. In other words Plato held that ideas have a reality of their own that was independent of our minds and souls. In Plato's philosophy we discover ideas and truths rather than creating them. So ideas like justice, virtue, and squaralarity are universal and eternal. Their true definitions are the same everywhere and for all eternity. Similar to the way instinct is for our survival. So is morality and justice just part of our instincts? When a little child does something wrong and then decides to lie about it to get out of the punishment is it nothing more than instincts? Did somebody teach your child to lie when they get into trouble so they could get out of the punishment? Did the child discover preexisting knowledge of how to lie to get out of trouble? If nobody is teaching the child how to lie, then where does the knowledge to lie come from? Is the knowledge to lie universal and eternal everywhere and for all time? Could Plato be correct in his philosophies?

Jean Piaget (1896-1980): Swiss psychologist, famous for his research of the development of reasoning in children. Piaget noticed in testing the intelligence of children that children often gave the same or very similar wrong answers at different ages. Through the careful studying of these results, Piaget came up with a philosophy concerning how reasoning develops and suggested that there are significant differences in our ability to reason at different ages. These findings are not attributed to the children's intelligence alone.

Piaget's work was the foundation for work in the areas of moral development and moral psychology. So if reasoning is not attributed to the intelligence alone it must somehow be preexisting knowledge. When you were a child how did you learn or decide to lie? So when you were a child did your mother say, "If you do something wrong tell me a lie and I'll see if I can catch you lying and we'll make a game out of it." Your mother could almost always catch you lying because when she was your age, she told the same lies. The exact same lies; that have been around, everywhere and eternally, for thousands of years. So Plato could in fact be right in his philosophy. Piaget later went on to study the differences of how children think and solve problems at different stages in their development.

John Stuart Mill (1806-1873) wrote the "Utilitarianism" philosophy of ethics, which later became to be known as the greatest happiness philosophy. Mill's said, "Actions are right in proportion as they tend to promote happiness. Being wrong as they tend to produce the reverse of happiness." So buying everybody at the bar a round of drinks would create the most happiness and therefore be morally correct to do so. I wish somebody with this philosophy were in the bar when I got there. By happiness, Mill means both the higher and lower sense of pleasures. High being intellect and lower meaning sensual. He considered these to be higher and lower because he believed that there is a human dignity that should urge us toward the intellectual over the sensual sides of pleasure. This philosophy on ethics is based on pleasure alone and doesn't really consider the reasoning part of ethics. So is sensual really only to be considered to be an animal or primal pleasure? Do animals have ethics?

Immanual Kant (1724-1804) stood in opposition to utilitarianism because Kant's philosophies on ethics centered on obligation regardless of consequences. Kant was interested in the question, "What is a moral action?" Not in who was or wasn't happy about it. To Kant it was clear that a moral action was one performed out of a sense of duty, rather than simply out of consideration or feeling or the possibility of some kind of reward for the person doing the act. If I give money to charity because I feel sorry for the needy rather than it's my duty to help the needy, then in Kant's philosophy I haven't done a moral act. I gave the money to charity to depress my feelings for the needy rather than because it's my duty to do so. If I give money to charity to gain popularity, then again, I'm not doing a moral act because I'm doing it to gain social acceptance. So to Kant the only possible moral act was one that was done out of a sense of duty and nothing else. The motive was far more important than the action it's self or the consequences of performing the duty. So to Kant in order to truly know if somebody acted morally or not you had to look at their intentions only and not the action it's self.

It's not enough to know that a Good Samaritan helped a person in need; we have to know exactly what his intentions were. The Samaritan might have thought he would be rewarded for his trouble or maybe the Samaritan felt sorry for the man because he went through the same problem last week. In Kant's philosophy the actions of the Good Samaritan were not moral because they weren't done out of a sense of duty. I agree to the fact that self-interest isn't the appropriate way to be motivated into a moral action. I personally disagree with the fact that whether or not somebody feels emotions like compassion is irrelevant to our moral assessment of his or her actions. Kant however would argue otherwise. Why do you think that would be so?

Kant concentrated so much on the intentions for an action rather than on the consequences because he believed that all people could in fact be moral. Since we can only be held accountable for things in our control and consequences of actions can at times be out of our control it's possible for good intentions to be misinterpreted as immoral. Let's say I'm walking down the street minding my own business. I see a man fall over grabbing at his chest and gasping, "My heart, my heart." I run over and try to do CPR to save his life but perform the CPR wrong and he dies anyhow. My intentions were good. I didn't run over there to speed up his process of dying. I was trying to save his life but failed to do so. My actions were morally correct but the consequence of not knowing what I was doing turned out to be tragic but not my intentions. We don't have complete control over our emotional reactions in dire emergencies so you shouldn't take emotions into consideration when determining some body's intentions as well. If morality was going to be universal and available to all human beings then Kant thought it had to rely entirely upon the will, in particularly on our sense of duty. Kant's philosophies on ethics had appeal that even an atheist could agree on.

Kant described the intention, which are behind any act as the maxim. The maxim is the principal underlying any action whether morally correct or not. For example the Good Samaritan could have the maxim, "Always help those in need if you feel sorry for them." or the maxim, "Always help those in need because you maybe rewarded for your troubles." However in Kant's philosophy the Samaritan should have had the maxim, "It's your duty to always help those in need." Then in Kant's philosophy the Good Samaritan committed a moral act. Just having any old maxim doesn't automatically make it moral. What if somebody had the maxim, "It's your duty to kill all criminals." If the person feels it's his duty does that make it morally correct?

Kant's philosophy said, "For any action to be considered a moral one the underlying maxim had to be a universal one." In other words everybody in your situation would've done the exact same thing you did. You shouldn't make an exception out of yourself either but should be impartial. So for example somebody stole office supplies at work and had the maxim, "It's okay to steal from work because they're not paying me enough." In order for this maxim to be considered moral everybody else in your same situation would have to agree with your maxim. I find it hard to believe everybody would considers stealing from work morally okay. That means that the maxim stealing from work is an immoral maxim because everybody in the same situation didn't agree with it. So the maxim didn't pass Kant's test.

Kant believed that as rational human beings we have certain duties. These duties were absolute and unconditional. Duties like you should always tell the truth or you shouldn't go around killing people and they apply regardless of the consequences of carrying them out. Kant thought morality was a system of commands to act a certain way and perform duties in a certain way. It's a version of the Golden Rules of Christianity. Where Christian ethics underline the duties of how to act a certain way. Maxims could also be turned around to benefit the person as well. How do you turn a maxim around?

If you don't want to go to prison, you should have the maxim, "Don't do bank robberies or you'll go to prison." If you want to be respected, "You should always tell the truth." Hypothetical duties tell you what you should or shouldn't do to achieve or avoid what you want to happen to you. Kant thought that one thing all maxims should have in common was, "Act only on maxims, which you can at the same time, want to be universal law." In other words, "Do onto others as you would want them to do onto you." Although Kant gave many different versions this is the most important of them and it has been immensely influential.

If somebody was living in the maxim, "Be a parasite and live off of other people." this maxim is immoral because if it were universal the parasites would run out of people to live on. Let's say I'm driving my car at 70 MPH in a 55MPH zone and I drive under a bridge and a state trooper gives me a ticket. The trooper had the maxim, "Give everybody speeding a ticket because it's my duty." Then the trooper is morally correct to do so. I do my duty and pay the ticket. The next day I drive under the same bridge and the same state trooper is trying to catch speeders. Let's say I'm driving 57 MPH in the 55MPH zone. This time the trooper didn't give me a ticket. Did the trooper fail to do his duty? Is the trooper immoral for not giving me a ticket? I was clearly over the speed limit so why didn't he give me a ticket? What if the trooper had the maxim; "People that are only two MPH over the speed limit might have something wrong with his or her speedometer and might not be intentionally speeding." If any other state trooper in his same situation has the same maxim, "The person might have something wrong with their speedometer." Then the trooper is morally correct because it's a universal maxim.

There was a man in New York City who witnessed a woman being raped by two men. The woman saw the man watching and called out to him for help. The man turned and walked away and didn't even call the police. The woman was badly beaten but pulled through okay. The police never found either rapist. The police did however find the man who didn't help her or call the police. The man had the maxim; "I don't know her and don't owe her anything." The police didn't arrest him because there wasn't a law against not reporting a crime. After word got around of what this man didn't do, every time he would go into a bar, restaurant, or store the owners of the businesses would ask him to leave and never come back. That means the maxim, "I don't owe you anything" didn't pass Kant's test and the maxim, "I don't want anybody that won't help a woman being raped in my business" is morally correct because it's a universal maxim.

In some state in America it's now a duty-based law to render aid to a car accident victim if you're the first car at the site of the accident. I believe it's called the Good Samaritan law. If you're driving along and come across a car wreck you must by law render aid. If you're a 95-year-old woman and can't rip the door open they expect you by law to drive to the nearest telephone and call the police, even if you have to drive 25 miles at your gas expense to do it. More and more states are adopting this duty-based law and I do in fact agree with it. How would you feel if you had a broken arm and bleeding in a smashed up car and people wouldn't stop to help you? I would've stopped and helped even if there wasn't a duty-based law. How do you feel about this new duty-based law?

During the Nazi Holocaust trials after World War two Hitler's henchmen gave the maxim, "I was only following orders when I killed millions of Jewish people." Let's put that to Kant's test. Do you think everybody who was in the same situation would have done exactly the same thing that they did? Does that maxim sound like it could be a universal law? Is that doing to others, as you would want them to do onto you? If you answered, "No" then guess what? You had the same maxim as the court did. Their maxim was, "You shouldn't have listened to Hitler and you're going to be executed for killing all those people because if you're stupid enough to listen to Hitler then we don't need your kind on the earth." Or well something like-that but the important thing is they're dead and gone.

What if a mad gunman came and knocked on my door and asked, "Where's your girlfriend I want to kill her." It's my duty to always tell the truth according to Kant and it's my duty regardless of the consequences. So do I say, "She's in the bedroom sleeping, please clean up when you're finished?" I have a duty to protect my girlfriend. So do I say, "She's not here right now can I take a message?" I would be immoral if I told a lie. I would be immoral if I fail to protect my girlfriend. So what do I do to be morally correct in Kant's philosophy? Kant's philosophy on universal laws quite clearly gives an answer, which corresponds with most everybody's unquestioned intuitions about right and wrong but not in every case.

One more of Kant's philosophies and I'll get off him. Kant said, "Treat other people as ends in themselves, and never as a means to an end." In other words don't use other people. The fact that they're individuals with wills and desires of his or her own; be sure to recognize his or her humanity. If somebody is pleasant to you because they want you to give them a job, then it's safe to assume he or she is using you as a means to get the job and not as a means in yourself. If somebody is pleasant to you because they truly like you, well that has nothing to do with ethics but it's nice to be liked. Reading Kant's philosophies is truly inspiring and I would like to recommend it to you as further reading if you're interested. Kant seemingly had answers for everything.

If well intentioned, idiots would unintentionally cause the deaths of a hundred people due to their incompetence? Would they be morally blameless because their intentions were good? If we judge them only on their intentions the only possible answer would be yes. Would you say that consequences in certain actions, is a worthy cause to judge somebody on, along with his or hers intentions? Consequentialism's philosophies believe that to judge if an action is right or wrong, don't just look at his or hers intentions but the consequences of the action as well. So if a mad gunman asked me where my girlfriend was? I could lie and send him off the trail and save my girlfriend's life. Consequentialism looks at the out come of my lie and not my intentions, even though my intentions were obvious to everybody.

Karl Marx (1818-1883): German political philosopher, and an inspiration to some forms of socialism. Marx believed social and economic forces shaped human thought. Things like our means of providing food, shelter, and other goods for ourselves, was the cause for the shaping of our thoughts and identities. It was Marx's philosophy that we must have social and economic justice in order to provide the conditions most befitting to human beings.

In 1848, Karl Marx and Friedrich Engels wrote "The Communist Manifesto" it was Marx's most famous work. The Communist Manifesto is a moral and political critique of capitalism and the false forms of socialism and a call to revolutionary action in order to improve the lives of the working people. Marx said, "Within capitalists societies human labor itself becomes a kind of capital to be bought and sold." People exchange his or her time and work for money. In Marx's mind people are exchanging a portion of their daily lives for money. Marx said, "There were many laborers but only a few people who owned most of the capital or the resources." The fact that the people who perform the most labor tented to reap the lowest rewards from their labor. Marx said, "Those who owned the means of production profited excessively at the expense of the working masses," Marx's philosophy was to treat people, as a commodity was to take away his or hers human dignity. So in Marx's mind he was being very ethical about the whole thing. Marx hoped that the revolution he foresaw would completely do away with philosophy and bring people back to the material realities that would define his or her humanity.

It was Marx's ultimate goal to start a Communist society in which the means of the people to live on was owned by all the people and private ownership would be abolished. People in the society would divide his or her days into thirds, one third of the time would be spent in the labor necessary to keep the community running, one-third on a job that the worker wants to work in, and one third going to school to get a higher education. Now everybody would have a share in the jobs to keep the community running and everybody could work in a field they were interested in and everybody could pursue a dream career by getting a higher education. Marx considered philosophy to be a class biased enterprise and had no use for it. Marx's work is known as Marxism and is considered a philosophy in the USA even though Marx considered his views to be more historical then philosophical. It's kind of poetic justice in it's own sick way. Marx didn't like philosophers yet he managed to be awarded the title of political philosopher. He didn't even read my book on "How to Think Like a Philosopher," what a smart guy.

I did in fact read The Communist Manifesto because anytime millions of people are willing to kill or die for a cause I'm curious to what that cause might be. So I walked into a capitalist's bookstore and bought The Communist Manifesto. Ironically it was wedged between The Constitution of the United States and The Declaration of Independence. Yes-sir-ree: anything for a laugh. I would recommend reading The Constitution and The Declaration it nice to see how it all comes together.

At the time that Marx wrote The Communist Manifesto there was no workmen's comp, forty-hour weeks, over time pay, or job safety. People were working 18-hours a day for whatever the mill wanted to pay. People were falling into the molten steel because they were so tired from working so many hours. Mills would have agreements with other mills so that if one mill paid so much the other mills would fall in line and pay the same wages. There was no safety in the mills. People were at the mercy of the mills they worked for. In the USA workers formed unions. Marx wanted to form a society. Even though it looks good on paper and there are some countries still practicing Communism, Communism has never achieved its ultimate goal.

Is selfishness ethical? A capital society thrives off selfishness. Does anybody really need a five thousand-dollar watch? Does anybody need a sports car to drive around? These items aren't necessary to our survival but they're necessary for the survival of a capitalist's society. Capitalist's societies are in fact driven by selfishness. That's why it's possible for somebody to become a millionaire. In a strange sort of way selfishness could be viewed as ethical. Selfishness can be carried away. People who want to make more money with no regards to other people's lives are selfish in an unnatural way. I knew and worked with a guy that had so much money it would take you three lifetimes to spend it all. Yet he wanted more and was willing to kill to get it. Never underestimate somebody else's greed. Could selfishness be a basic animal instinct?

A hungry lion in the jungle runs into a herd of zebras and jumps on one to try and kill it. All the other zebras runaway and leave the one being attacked by the lion on it's own. The zebras have the Maxim, "If you're attacked by a lion you're on your own." All the other zebras seemingly agree with that maxim making it morally correct. However if all the zebras would start kicking the lion as hard as they could, to get the lion off the other zebra, they could in fact save the zebra's life. If all the zebras had the maxim, "Lets all work together to fight off lions." They would have a much better chance of survival as a group instead of by themselves. If I was a lion and had fifty zebras kicking me as hard as they could, I would give it up and look for something else to eat. Let's say the lion killed the zebra in two seconds, if all the zebras would still kick the lion so the lion couldn't eat the zebra the lion would still learn to leave zebras alone and wouldn't attack zebras anymore. Lions are Kings of the jungle but I don't care how big and bad you are fifty zebras would be a handful. Nevertheless zebras will runaway without helping their fellow zebra. Sometimes they'll run till they feel out of danger and turn around to watch the lion eat or carry off the zebra that was killed. How can people use animal ethics?

I read in a newspaper that there was a woman being savagely raped by a sick man. During the rape the man, I guess do to over confidence, lied the gun he had on the table to take his shirt off. The woman simply reached over and picked up the gun and emptied the gun into the rapist. So the woman had the maxim, "It's okay to kill for survival just like lions kill for survival." Every other woman in her same situation would've done the same thing so she was morally correct in her actions. If a lion was raping a zebra and the lion put his gun on the table do you think the zebra would've grabbed the gun?

There was a person I knew who had a drug dealer for a boyfriend. I told her when they raid a drug house they take the piano player too. She made countless attempts to persuade him from dealing drugs. He flat dabbed refused to give it up. So one day the lion police showed up and took everybody to jail. She was the piano player and got caught in the same snare that the drug dealer was caught in. So if somebody doesn't have enough commonsense to not deal drugs then you have to let the lion police have that zebra. Every zebra for them selves, if you can't talk some sense into a person, who is in the wrong, then you must let nature take its coarse. So it's okay to think everybody for them selves if they won't listen to you. So animal ethics or instincts can be practiced by people, however, it's a shame to compare humans with animals. You are responsible for your mind and actions only and nobody else's. So it's easy to see why it's possible to use some animal ethics in our life.

Euthanasia: also known as mercy killing. It's an attempt to bring a quick and painless death to people or animals that are sick or suffering. The moral ethics behind euthanasia is for the justification to end needless suffering in a person or animal that is going to die anyhow. Euthanasia normally arises when somebody or animal is terminally ill and suffering. Euthanasia is divided into two parts. First is known as active, which is the deliberate cause of death similar to murder. An active euthanasia would be like somebody else shooting the person or animal and causing them to die. Second is passive where you let nature take it's coarse. A passive euthanasia would be like a doctor pulling the plug on a life support machine and the person or animal will die due to its illness rather than murdered.

I truly believe that there are things worse than death. Being paralyzed from the neck down to me would be worse than death. If all I could do were move my head side to side and nothing else, I would be a piece of furniture with a mind. I couldn't work to support myself or go to the bathroom on my own. If I didn't cry myself to death first, I would want to be killed. I wouldn't want to be a couch potato the rest of my life. It would be like being dead anyway but the only difference is I would know I was dead. So euthanasia could be considered to be ethical in a way. What do you think about mercy killing?

Passive euthanasia has made its way into the American code of ethics. In nursing homes across America they sometimes practice passive Euthanasia. When an old person checks into a nursing home he or she maybe asked to sign a contract saying, "If you go into a heart attack or start to die from your illness do you want us to revive you or let nature take its coarse and let you die?" If the person signs the contract to let them die if they're having a heart attack then the nursing home will not try and save his or her life, if they start to have a heart attack. In theory if the person was in his or her home and had a heart attack and nobody was around to help they would die. So is that different than nurses knowing somebody is having a heart attack and do nothing to help because they signed a contract? Is it murder to let somebody die if you have the know how to save his or her life? The person is dying of natural causes anyway. We all should die of natural causes so is it murder to willingly let somebody die? In order for this to be moral it must pass Kant's test. If everybody in the same situation would do the same thing then it's moral to let it happen. If letting somebody die is the same thing you would want other people to do onto you then it's moral. So in your eyes did it pass Kant's test? It did pass for me.

Passive euthanasia is more excepted because the person does die of natural causes. Aids, cancer, and old age do in fact kill people naturally. So people feel that the person or animal would've died naturally. If something dies naturally nobody is really to blame for the death. People feel better about passive euthanasia than active because nature is out of our control and we're only responsible for our minds and actions and not what naturally happens. Passive euthanasia is becoming more and more accepted each day by more and more nursing homes across America and Canada. The people themselves, who suffer form the terminal illness are also agreeing to the passive euthanasia philosophy to end his or her torment and suffering.

I was watching a movie one night with my girlfriend. The movie was about this man who broke his neck and ended up paralyzed from the neck down. All he could move was his head and he could talk. The movie went on to show the family trying to deal with the handicapped man. The movie was in fact inspiring to see the will to conquer his handicap. My girlfriend said, "I don't think I could stand being paralyzed like that." I said, "You wouldn't have to stand it for long." With a puzzled look she asked, "What do you mean?" "If you were paralyzed from the neck down and couldn't move anything but your head I would kill you." "If you killed me you would go to prison for life." "Yes if they could catch me. I've never killed anybody before but I already know if you want to be a murderer, golden rule number one is, absolutely positively don't let anybody ever catches you kill somebody. I'm a pretty smart guy and can pull it off." She sat up to look me in the eyes better and asked, "What if I don't want you to kill me?" "I guess you better fight me off then." "If I'm paralyzed I couldn't fight you off." I said, "You catch on quick." She jumped up and gave me an earful and marched out of my house slamming the door behind her. The conversation didn't go as smoothly as I would've liked but my intentions were clear.

The very next day she called me on the phone to end her masquerade of what a bad boy I was and to give me an apology for all the things she said to me the previous night. She moved in with me two weeks later and we lived together for six months. She never broke her neck or became paralyzed but she did start saying, "Love has nothing to do with logic." She also accused me of talking about thing in to much depth and making big deals out of what people say and do. "Huh, can you imagine that?" Where do you think she got that hair brained idea? What mountain, which molehill? Nevertheless she moved in with me knowing what my intentions were if she became paralyzed from the neck down and couldn't commit suicide on her own.

There was a certain doctor, who will remain nameless, that was gallivanting around the USA helping terminally ill or severely handicapped people commit suicide. He became to be known as doctor death. If somebody was paralyzed from the neck down and could only move their head they were incapable of committing suicide on his or her own. So this person would contact doctor death and ask him to assist in helping them commit suicide. How they can operate a telephone if they're paralyzed is beyond me. Then the good doctor would rig some kind of machine that could be triggered by the paralyzed person's mouth so the person could in fact pull the trigger and commit suicide. Example the doctor could put poison in a small glass tube and place the tube into the mouth of the paralyzed person and if the person wants to commit suicide they simply bite down on the tube breaking the glass and release the poison.

Active euthanasia is looked down upon because it is very similar to murder. Active euthanasia is somebody causing the death of a person or animal by shooting, stabbing, or drowning. Active euthanasia is causing death other than by natural means. Murder is causing death by other than natural means. So they're considered to be one in the same by some people. Suicide is also causing death but is also looked down upon as a sin. People who decide to sign a contract with a nursing home to let them die if they're have a heart attack or whatever are some times viewed as committing suicide but not as often as people who do in fact commit suicide.

Suicide could possibly be viewed as active euthanasia. A person that commits suicide may in fact believe that they're putting them selves out of his or her misery. In all most every country suicide is viewed as being a sin or a cowards way out of life. Nobody wants to be associated with a person who committed suicide. Even at my cousin's eulogy at the church they insinuated that he didn't know the gun was loaded. Even though the police who found his body in front of the fire department also found a suicide note. Like somebody's really going to look down the barrel of a gun and pull the trigger to see if it's loaded or not. He knew perfectly well what he was doing and did it anyway. Nobody fully stands behind the approval of suicide.

People who sign a contract at the nursing home are in some sort of a way committing suicide. The reason people don't really view it that way is because the person dies of passive euthanasia. If the person starts to go into a heart attack the nurses let them go and die naturally without giving them any aid. Even on the death certificate it'll say death due to heart attack. When friends and family ask, "How did they die" the first thing out of his or her mouth is they died of a heart attack. They're not going to say, "Well they died of passive euthanasia because they signed a contract saying not to give them any aid if they start to die." The life insurance won't pay on suicides so passive euthanasia is more acceptable nowadays.

The big issue with euthanasia is why or how do we determine if it's ethical or moral? The first thing to ask our selves is what is having or owning a life? What is the definition of having a life? Is having a life nothing more than having a heart beating in our chest? Somebody paralyzed from the neck down has that. Is having a life owning a health mind? Somebody paralyzed from the neck down has that. Yet, nobody wants to live life paralyzed from the neck down. If somebody paralyzed from the neck down believed that to own a life was simply to have a health mind then this person wouldn't want to die. Every individual has their-own personal definition of what owning or having a life is. If their definition of what life is changes or is changed by uncontrollable circumstances then they'll consider euthanasia.

My personal definition of having a life is being independent and having interaction with the external world. If I was paralyzed from the hip down and had full use of my arms and mind I would continue on and still have or own a life. I wouldn't want to die. If I was paralyzed from the neck down and could only move my head, I would want and seek euthanasia. I couldn't live life not being able to support myself, feed myself, or even go to the bathroom by myself. I would not consider myself to have or own a life. I would be a burden to whoever was taking care of me. I would be a plant with eyes or a piece of furniture that talks but I wouldn't consider myself to be a human being but only a worthless burden to some poor family member. I would also be incapable of committing suicide on my own. If somebody would come along and offer me help I would accept it and give them everything I own to help me end my misery. I would be scared but I would agree to what ever plan they had and be grateful for it. How do you feel about that? Would you help me if I asked you to? If you were in the same situation would you consider it yourself? Would you ask me to help you if you were paralyzed from the neck down? Would you consider paralyzed from the neck down as having or owning a life?

Everybody's definition is different of what owning a life is. A man committed suicide because his girlfriend left him. So maybe his definition was I only have a life if this certain girl is my lover. The Japanese Kamikazes killed them selves rather than be captured by Americans in world war two. So their definition of having a life must have been not being a prisoner of war. People have committed suicide because they have chronic pains. To own a life means not being in constant pain. People have committed suicide over cars, money, lovers, prison sentences, and you name it. All of these things have one thing in common. All of them were perceived as unacceptable to be considered owning or having a life by these people. So is suicide euthanasia?

If we started life as nothing more than a sperm cell and there are at the very least one million sperm cells released at the same time, then you've very lucky my friend. You were the one and only sperm cell that found the egg and got into the egg. You won the most important Easter egg hunt of your life. You beat out literally millions of your brothers and sisters to get into that egg and start the wonderful process of life. That's like a two million to one shot. That's like winning the state lottery. Do you consider yourself lucky? You're a winner and didn't even know it. Yet, people through his or her life away with suicide for some of the dumbest reasons.

I find it very hard to believe that a person thinks that the definition of life is a certain car, lover, you name it, is to own or have a life. It sickens me to no end to hear of people committing suicide over some of the stupidest things in the world but yet people do it every day. To even put euthanasia into perspective we must have a universal definition of what life is. People that commit suicide we don't have any control over. People we practice active euthanasia on we do. Until we have a universal definition of exactly what having or owning a life is, then how can we make active euthanasia ethically or morally correct? Until that definition is in fact found we're going to practice active euthanasia to what we describe or believe what owning or having a life is on somebody else who may not have the same views as us. So that's what makes active euthanasia immoral and unethical.

The death penalty is more than likely against the will of the person being executed. I support the death penalty fully. We can't have murderers out killing people anytime they please. Does executing a killer punish the killer or protect us? The death penalty has been around for thousands of years and guess what? It's still here in the new millennium. I don't believe anybody has been executed so far but I'm thinking they will.

Some states have capitol murder and first-degree murder. First-degree murder is when you make a plan to kill somebody and then carry it out. Second-degree murder is you didn't plan on killing somebody but ended up doing it anyhow. Example your in a fist fight with somebody and in the heat of battle you pickup a chair and hit them with it and they die. Capitol murder is when you kill a policeman, an elected official, or you kill somebody while committing a felony crime. It's capitol murder even if you didn't plan to kill a policeman or not. The punishment for capitol murder is life in prison with absolutely no chance for parole ever or the death penalty. The punishment for first-degree murder is 10-40 years or life in prison with chance of parole. So why is the life of a policeman worth more punishment than killing me? That's my biggest question. The punishment should be the same whether somebody killed the president of the United States or a bum living under a bridge. What punishment should a killer receive for killing somebody you loved very deeply?

As for the condemned I feel they shouldn't have to suffer as they're being executed. I have no problem with lethal injection style execution. Nor do I care if they do feel it or feel scared that they're being executed. I think the death penalty is ethical and morally correct because I think it is a deterrent to murder. I've heard people say, "The death penalty isn't a deterrent for murder." Yet, nobody has ever said, "You're lucky this state has the death penalty because if they didn't I would've killed three or four different people." How can we really know how many murders the death penalty has deterred from happening? I still believe the death penalty is an important crime deterrent and should still be practiced. What do you think?

Exploitation or taking advantage of the weakness or vulnerability of a person, group, or thing for the benefit of another in a way that is not in the best interests of that person, group, or thing. The best know exploitation artists are Adolf Hitler and Karl Marx. Marx said, "That capitalism is inherently exploitative because it concentrated everything a worker needs to survive, except the worker's labor, in the hands of a small number of elites." The elites then ensure that the worker's are vulnerable by creating unemployment through labor saving technologies. The unemployment in turn creates a pool of unemployed people who are starving to work for anything just so they can survive, and this drives all the wages down. The system is exploitative because the elites use a weakness or vulnerabilities of the workers or the overabundance of labor due to the high unemployment, to take advantage of them by taking profits that overwhelmingly exceed the elites own contribution to the production. It was Marx's intention to point this out and turn it around to get the people on his side.

Adolf Hitler developed or practiced colonialism which is rich countries exploiting poorer ones. Hitler exploited Poland to no end. Unlike Marx, Hitler used military tactics to exploit whatever he could from whomever he could. Exploitation is one of the most unethical and immoral thing anybody could possible do. Blackmailers are normally the lowest possible exploiters on the face of the earth. They hid like rats trying to collect the money that they're exploiting off of some misguided individual. People have committed suicide over being blackmailed yet exploiters always seemingly get away clean.

Children porno exploiters make movies of children having sex or being naked on film so they can sell it on the black-market. They're hard to catch because the sick people who actually buy the films keep them under lock and key or keep them some place other than where they live. They know if they get caught with such films, nobody will forgive them. Their maxim, "Child porno is forbidden." Is also shared by millions of people. So they know if they get caught they're going to lose a lot of friends. Yet, they still buy these films. I don't have the answer for why. I can only wonder if they're doing this to children as well.

Some women exploit men for their money. They'll go with a guy and let him think they really love them but the truth is they're only after his money. Sugar daddies spend lots of money on their young girlfriends, yet some still have a wife at home who truly loves him. Some times a man will also exploit a woman as well getting her to buy him stuff or have abnormal sex to satisfy his desire for a mistress. The people being exploited somehow know that's what's going on, yet they choose to ignore it. By them choosing to ignore it, the exploiter is now invited to exploit them even more.

I've seen cases with my own eyes of abusive husband exploiting his wife. The wife can't get a job on her own to make enough money to support herself and her children so she feels trapped into living with the abusive husband. The husband acknowledges that fact and uses it against his wife even more. He'll say, "If you don't straighten out I'll throw you out into the streets." Exploiting the fact that he knows, that she knows, she doesn't have a career that could support her and her children. By him doing so he exploits more and more self-esteem off of her until she loses the desire to even try. This gives him even more control over her, which means he can now exploit until his heart is content. Yep, he now has the idea that the skies the limit.

Exploitation is by far the easiest crime to stop. If you're being black-mailed because you did something wrong and they'll turn you in if you don't pay. Go and confess to the act you did wrong to the right person and reap your rewards. If somebody's using you because you have money, dump him or her. Anybody you can pick up with a shinny new sports car, you can pick up with a six-pack of beer and I know because I've done it. If you feel you have to live with somebody who is abusive, you're wrong. It's better to work two jobs than to let somebody exploit you. It's better to eat peanut-butter sandwiches for a month then to let somebody exploit you. It's actually better to live under a bridge than to let somebody exploit you. In order to think like a philosopher you must see how easy it is to stop the crime of exploita-tion. You do not have to let anybody exploit you ever. Please stop the insanity. If you learn nothing else from this book, please acknowledge this; "Never let anybody exploit you." It will only get worse. I know this because it was my mother who I was talking about who felt trapped by her abusive husband who relentlessly and without any mercy exploited my mother down to zero self-esteem. It took my mother years to finally acknowledge her self-esteem again and I kid you not. If you ignore me you're going to spend the rest of your life grabbing your ankles. The definition of insanity is doing the same thing over and over again and expecting a different result.

If a woman was raped even if it only took one hour to rape her, she'll be devastated for years and the rapist could be sentenced to life in prison. An abusive husband could exploit his wife for years making her do sexual acts she didn't want to do and slapping her around call-ing her names and taking all of her self-esteem and dignity away. Yet, he won't even get as much as a ten-dollar fine. The wife as well as the woman who was raped will be devastated for years while the abusive husband is free to search for a new victim to exploit. Why is it that criminals who exploit people get away with his or her crime? It's like we sweep the actions of the exploiter under the rug and try and keep it out of view of our friends and family. If a man rapes a woman we don't sweep his actions under the rug but look for justice in our court system. So why should the exploiter not be brought to justice as well? People say, "Well the woman should have known better than to let him do that to her." So should the woman who's a victim of a rape have known better as well? By saying this we can push aside the crime of exploitation and forgive the exploiter so that the exploiter is welcomed again to search out a new victim to exploit.

Men get exploited too, by woman who are only after their money. The men think that by buying her everything she wants she'll hang around and maybe see what a in creditable guy he is and fall madly in love with him and he won't have to keep spending his money on her anymore. Life should be so simple. You can never satisfy the greed of an exploiter. You'll spend thousands and she won't want to stay with you. The man will think, "I've got thousands invested in her so I better not quite now or all that money was for nothing." So the man will dig deeper into his pockets and spend even more money in the belief, "She'll see what a great guy I am any second now." Well Mr. Fool and his money, that time will never come in your lifetime. One day the light of the real reality will come crashing in on the man and he'll simply break it off with the woman who's exploiting him. Once again the exploitation criminal will be free to go because the man more than likely isn't going to go through the embarrassment of exposing the exploitation criminal and confess to the world that he was a sucker. So the exploiting woman is free to find her next victim, which is another man with a pocketful of money.

People always do what is necessary to achieve his or her goals. People who sell computers do so because it's profitable. People open restaurants because other people will come and eat there, making it profitable. People will always do whatever is necessary to achieve his or her goals of getting what they want in the external world, especially so in America. Where there's this illusion of always having to have everything imaginable. Somebody wouldn't open a business called, "The Great Natural Paper Weight Company." Then go door-to-door trying to sell rocks that they found in a ditch. They wouldn't be able to sell any so therefore it would be a waste of his or her time and resources. Trying to sell a rock, as a natural paperweight wouldn't work, so to do so is a waste of time. People will only do what will achieve his or her goals.

I was in a toy store with my niece and she saw a toy she liked and said, "Uncle Frank, I would really like to have that toy." She was nine at the time. I pick up the toy from the shelf and was looking for the age requirements on the box and she said, "If you loved me, you would buy that toy for me." I immediately put the toy back on the shelf and said, "We are leaving the store." If I had bought the toy after she said, "If you loved me, you would buy it for me." Then I would've invited her to do it again because she would have the maxim; "If I want Uncle Frank to buy or do something for me, all I have to do is threaten to not love him anymore." If I allow that maxim to be morally correct that means she has a new tool to exploit me with so she can achieve her goals of getting what she wants. People do whatever works to achieve his or her goals of getting what they want in the external world. By me not allowing her to exploit me her maxim of, "All I got to do is threaten Uncle Frank to stop loving him and he'll do what I want." If it doesn't work she's not going to go door-to-door selling rocks because it's a waste of time.

Is it possible that the children who were able to successfully exploit his or her Uncles or parents grew up to be the exploiters that are out there today? Is that why we have a society of socially accepted exploiters? A little girl who successfully exploited her parents or Uncles believes that the crime of exploitation does in fact work in achieving his or her goals of getting what he or she wants and even if it doesn't work there's really not that much punishment if it doesn't, then why not do it? Why not take a shot at exploiting somebody? If it doesn't work on one person there's always another to try it on or maybe put a new twist on the tactic and tries a new angle to exploit somebody on. People do what they know will work its just that simple. If a parent allows his or her child to exploit them or thinks it's cute that they tried to exploit them then why not practice exploitation? If it works in your childhood why wouldn't it work in your adulthood?

If a little girl could get away with exploiting to achieve her goals then why should she give it up in her adulthood? Could the little girl who exploited her family be the woman who exploits money from men who believe that their generosity will convince the woman to fall in love with them? Is the little girl who did exploit, grow up to be the women who exploits men for their money? People do whatever works to achieve his or her goals of getting what they want in the external world. Could the little boy who exploits his family grow up to be the abusive husband who exploits his wife? Could the little boy who's successful in exploiting his family grow up to be the rapist who exploits a woman? Adolf Hitler proved that guns and power are tools for exploiting. So the young boys who go on shooting sprees, using a new tactic on the well-known tool of exploitation? If somebody pointed a gun at you, could they exploit you? If you think it's cute for a little boy or girl to threaten to stop loving you if you don't buy them a toy, then how will the child know that it's socially not acceptable to exploit people?

In order to think like a philosopher you must realize that exploitation is exploitation. There is no such thing as different levels of exploitation. There is no acceptable level of exploitation. If exploiting your wife is acceptable and it's acceptable because the wife allows it to happen then why isn't it acceptable for a rapist to exploit a woman as well? Is it possible for a little harmless exploitation to escalate into a more unacceptable level of exploitation? Is this the reason we have teenage cop killers? The teenager took the exploitation to a higher level because the lower levels worked so well. What is your expectation of what an acceptable level of exploitation is? Where do you draw the line on being exploited?

Can exploitation ever be acceptable or morally or ethically correct? The answer is yes. The United States of America has laws that you must follow. Instead of America saying, "If you love your country you'll follow our laws." They say, "Follow our laws or you'll be sent to prison." Follow our laws or go to prison. "Hum, sounds like exploitation to me." As Americans we accept this exploitation because it makes sense to us. It is in fact moral to have consequences to crimes otherwise people would do crimes. So if it's acceptable to use exploitation to uphold the law but does it somehow give the illusion that it's okay to exploit to get people to do what you want them to? Is that why so-called lower levels of exploitation are in fact acceptable? Is it possible that an abusive husband is nothing more than somebody who misinterpreted exploitation rules of how we uphold the law in America is? Do you believe it's okay to exploit consequences for breaking the law? "I sure do." I wonder if this has anything to do with why we accept exploitation in the first place. Until people are willing to follow the laws without being threatened by imprisonment America will in fact have to keep the exploitation of, if you break a law you go to prison. Until that time people must, as philosophers and small business managers, determine what is acceptable and what is clearly not acceptable as far as exploitation goes. If you learn nothing else from this book, please acknowledge, "Don't let anybody exploit you against your will." Just by simply learning that it'll compensate you for the small price you've paid for this book.

Hate Crimes or acts of violence or destruction motivated by prejudice or other forms of racism. Many counties now have laws imposing higher than normal sentences for hate crimes. Hate crimes are viewed as more reprehensible than normal crimes because it is effectively an offense against a group of people rather than just one individual. Hate crimes have the effect of breeding fear into members of the target group of people, taking away his or her dignity as well as inviting other prejudice people to commit similar acts of violence. Many hate crime acts have started out to be small acts of violence that later snowballed out of control similar to Communism has. In Nazi Germany simple acts of hate crime motivated into what became to be known as the Holocaust. The swastikas the Nazi's whore clearly identified them as hate criminals and their philosophies on a perfect order. The courts do in fact have harsher sentences for truly heinous crimes but people who stand for the group that didn't actually committed the crime are free to walk around holding the fear of his or her group over the heads of the target victims the group opposes. How could that possible be fair? Is it possible to put a stop to it?

If I belong to a bowling league and somebody in the league commits bank robbery should everybody on the league go to prison as well? Should all the banks live in fear of somebody in my bowling league coming into the bank? Yet, if we have a group of white Nazis and only one kills an opposing person only he goes to prison. All the rest are able to threaten and torment the family of the victim at will with no punishment. They're allowed to show his or her swastikas and go wherever they please. Yet, if they didn't break the law they can't go to prison but somehow that seems unfair. Should anybody who's involved with the group also go to prison because they shared the same philosophies that the real killer had? If that was the case then if somebody on my bowling league committed a crime you could also say, "Frank's part of that group too so let's send him to prison as well." Is bank robbery a hate crime? Did the bank robber hate the bank he was robbing?

Bank robbery is a serious crime but hardly qualifies as a hate crime. Hate crimes I believe should be viewed as what they are nothing more than an enemy of the United States to which doesn't deserve any mercy from our government. Groups of Nazis should be considered nothing more than an enemy power trying to over through our government in a time of war. In my opinion there is nothing wrong with making the entire group prisoners of war for life or until they have a country that is strong enough in power to forcibly take them out of the United States prison system against the United States' will. To which I say good luck.

Greed and excessive desires to acquire wealth, money, and even personal attention. A greedy person may still be miserly accumulating excessive wealth for no apparently other reason than to simple hoard whatever he or she have. It is generally seen as wrong because like any craving, the desire is so strong that it overwhelms other considerations, like dignity and decency, and therefore may possibly lead to criminal and other immoral acts. The power of greed is so strong in the desires that it tends to overwhelm the ability for someone to develop his or her areas of interpersonal relationships. Greed also has a place on our good side of ethics as well.

A capitalist's society runs on greed and selfishness. People don't need supper sonic sports cars, cell phones, or diamonds to survive. The company that sells them needs you to buy them so they can survive. People some times make a living off of make things they don't want or need to sell to people who do want or need them. Free marketing is how capital society supports its self. The capital society is very ethical in a sense because everybody has a right to pursue whatever pleasures they wish. There is nothing wrong with buying your own home or car. The kicker is that in order for somebody to feel successful is to buy a great big house or car. Then they some times bite off more than they can chew on the payments. So they work harder to try and get the money and feel cheated because they have to work harder so they buy themselves something even more on credit to compensate for them having to working harder. It does in fact start off slow and works it's way into bankrupts then the real fun starts.

My sister is a nurse that worked in a nursing home for years. She's has been along side many deathbeds. She has yet to hear somebody dying on his or her deathbed say, "You know, I should've worked more over time so I could've bought that supper sonic sports car and drove it before I died." What she normally heard them say, "I wished I spent more time with my family rather than working all that overtime." So once again philosophers, we're asking what exactly is having a life? Can you live without the supper sonic car of your dreams for more time with your family? Is it un-American to drive anything less than the supper sonic car of your dreams? After all what will the neighbors think? Maybe nobody will want to date you if your not driving the supper sonic car. I mean what kind of American are you anyway? Chase the pie in the sky my friends just don't forget to look down every now and then so you don't trip over the rest of us.

We as American are bombarded with advertisements. We can't get our mail without some sort of junk mail being in there. If I would take all the junk mail and glue it all together I would have a tree. It's very hard to watch TV because they have one commercial on right after another with no mercy what so ever. We have very little peace of mind from the constant bombardment of ads and salespeople who try and get our attention at every chance they get. I got a call from a man right in the middle of dinner one night and he wanted to know if I needed a replacement window for my car. I told him that if I broke my car's window I would have enough commonsense to call for a replacement window and wouldn't wait for somebody to call and ask me. If I go to a public restroom there's an ad right above the urinal advertising something. If Americans are constantly bombarded by how important it is to buy everything imaginable no wonder our kids have the idea that money is power. This illusion is so strong that money is power that people commit suicide if they feel they're not rich enough. How absurd is this?

Knowledge is power. Things that you believe to be true you consider to be knowledge. I'm a philosopher. I have the knowledge of the different philosophies and I believe them to be true. Because of my knowledge of reality I can't be mislead. I live life in the real reality and never push aside my preexisting knowledge to adopt a make believe sense of reality to avoid going through all the hassles involved with dealing with the problems I encounter. Because of my knowledge of logic and reasoning people regard my opinion with the utmost highest respect. I look at new problems as exciting new challenges instead of new headaches that I have to deal with. I know I can achieve my goals regardless of how high I set them because I know I can reason them out with my preexisting knowledge of logic. With my knowledge of the human mind I can see people's intentions like I'm looking through a plate glass window. Bigots and narrow-minded people run screaming for cover when I walk into a room. Philosophy is like a breath of fresh air that blows away all the cloudy haze that some times blurs our vision. With my knowledge of ethics and morality people regard me with having virtue and high character as in a gentleman. I can make decisions on how to act with my knowledge of ethics. I have an inner peace by knowing I'll always be okay because I can take on anything. If you could feel the inner peace of what confidence can give you, you would run to your nearest bookstore to buy every philosophy book that wasn't nailed down. I can't recommend it enough my friends.

Best of all; its all yours for the taking. I have what I need and need what I have. I didn't learn what I have from watching sitcoms on TV. I have it because I pursued it. If you're looking for more control in your life I can't recommend philosophy and small business management enough. It would be in your best interest not to snub your nose up at what I'm telling you. If you could only feel for one minute the confidence that I feel every day you would understand what I'm talking about.

Once again I ask, "What do we define as having or owning a life?" Every one us have our own opinion of what the answer to that simple question is. I live very simple and don't own very many things yet, I have no trouble what so ever finding friends or ladies who wish to spend time with me. We go out camping and roast hotdogs and marshmallows on a campfire and we go on picnics in the woods in the summer and have lots of cookouts. To me these are the thing's that makes life worth living. The examined life is the only life worth living. When I'm with my friends we talk about real issues not about soap operas or other TV sitcoms. I have an inner peace with myself too. What do I mean by inner peace? I'm not bombarded by TV ads. Being constantly bombarded by unimportant issues confuses people who try and not miss any of it. Inner peace is sitting quietly and thinking about what's important to you. There has been many a nights when it was me, a bottle of wine, and whatever was in my head. I'm here to tell you it makes for some great therapy. Take this idea for a test drive and let me know how it worked out for you.

This concludes this chapter on business ethics. Ethics and morality is the epitome of what we are as a society and as individuals. You can certainly tell a lot of an individual as well as a society by what morals and ethics are important to them. Until there is a well-established universal code of ethics we as human beings are responsible for determining what is right and what is wrong. We all have our own version of what a perfect world should be. We also have our own version of what having or owning a life is to us. All that glitters isn't gold but only an illusion of what people believe to be true. It's the Inner Light that is naked to the eye that gives off the glowing essence of peace that others fail to pursue. We as human beings can put a man on the moon but yet we cannot find the will to educate the ignorant, we're only responsible for our own mind and actions and for nobody else's or will some force hold us accountable for mankind?

Chapter Eight

Basic Business Logic

Logic is to philosophy and business management what mathematics is to science. In a way logic is mathematics and mathematics is logic. Logic's definition is a science concerned with the principals of valid reasoning and correct inference, either inductive or deductive. Basic reasoning, with universal knowledge of things you believe to be true. The purpose of logic is to make explicit the rules by which inferences may be drawn, rather than to study the actual reasoning processes that people use, which may or may not confirm to the same rules. In other words logical answers need very little if any explanations. There are to types of logic inductive and deductive. Deductive logic, in which a conclusion follows from a set of premises or propositions, is different than inductive logic, which studies the way in which propositions may support a conclusion without entailing it.

Deductive logic the conclusion can't be wrong if the premises are true. In order for us to start there are some terms I should review with you. Inductive: Pertaining to or result from induction. Induce: Other influences or cause actions. Deduce: Take away from or deduct from. Deduction: The act of deducing reasoning from the general to the particular. Reasoning from stated premises to logical conclusions. Premises: A proposition that serves as a ground for argument or for a conclusion. Proposition: Proposal offered for consideration. It could be any matter or any person to be dealt with. Predicate: To found or base on or to state or affirm concerning the subject of the proposition or predicate of the proposition. I've decided to talk and teach logic in its most basic sense. I'm going to write about deductive and inductive logic as well as good old commonsense. Once these techniques are mastered you'll never look at problems the same way again. Understanding logic will in its own sense give you a more confident feeling while you're pursuing your goals in life.

Aristotle (384BC-322BC) is generally recognized as the first great logician. Aristotle's philosophy is called syllogism. Syllogism or categorical syllogism is the influence of one proposition from two premises. For example all mice have tails; all things with tails are four legged; so all mice are four legged. Each premise has one term in common with the conclusion and one term in common with the other premises. The major premise of the syllogism is the premise containing the predicate of the proposition. The minor premise contains its own subject. So the first premise of the example is the minor premise, the second is the major premise, which is in the conclusion, and having a tail is the middle term, which doesn't occur in the conclusion. This is just lightly touching base on Aristotle's syllogism philosophy but syllogism has been practiced until around the 1900, before giving way to a philosophy called syllogistic. If you're interested in learning more you shouldn't have any trouble finding a book on Aristotle's syllogism in any bookstore or library. This chapter is only going to look at the fundamentals of logic. However this will be interesting to the small business manager and philosophy beginner.

Proposition: People who go over the speed limit get speeding tickets. The subject is speeding tickets. Premise: People who obey the speed limit don't get any speeding tickets. Middle term but still has something in common with minor. Predicate of the proposition: It's good not to get any speeding tickets or in other words obey the speed limit and you won't have any trouble. Here's an example for somebody who dropped out of school. Proposition: A GED is equal to a high school diploma. Premise: People with high school diplomas get higher paying jobs. Predicate of the proposition: It's good for a high school drop out to get a GED. Normally logical considerations don't end in three sentences. It's a complicated world with some complicated premise out there. Now that we have a small grasp on logic let's put it to a real test. These methods will come in handy as a small business owner or manager.

There was a woman who burned some steaks on the outdoor grill so badly that they couldn't be eaten. Her abusive husband slapped her in the face and said, "See what you made me do. If you had half a brain I wouldn't have to knock some sense into you. Steaks cost money, don't waste my hard earned money." Proposition: You should leave anybody who slaps you and talks to you like you're garbage. Deduction: If I don't burn anymore of the steaks he won't slap me. Premise: Do you think it's okay to slap people who have unintentionally burned some steaks? Deduction: No, but maybe he was only having a bad day. I don't want to throw away my marriage over one mistake. Premise: Has your husband ever hit you before or talked to you like you're trash? Deduction: Yes, but he only does that then he's having a bad day. Premise: Do you feel trapped in the marriage because you have no career to support yourself and your children if you move out? Deduction: My husband has a good job and can easily support us. All I have to do is just be a better wife that's all. Premise: Your husband is taking advantage of you and your situation and exploiting the fact that you believe you can't leave and support you and your children. Induction: You know it's not acceptable to slap somebody who burned some steaks. Induction: You're pushing away your preexisting knowledge of it's wrong to slap people for no good reason. Induction: You know it would be a hassle to pack up all your stuff and try and make it on your own. So you push aside your preexisting knowledge and make up the make believe reality that if I simply don't burn anymore of the steaks I'll be okay. Induction: You know he's not going to quit but things are only going to get only worse each time he gets away with hitting you. Predicate of the proposition: She can't push aside her preexisting knowledge to avoid all the hassles of trying to make it on her own by making up a different reality that if she simply becomes a better wife the abusive husband will magically stop hitting her.

Illogical answers are usually punch lines that are used in telling jokes. How many people does it take to screw in a light bulb? Ten, one, to hold the light bulb and nine, to turn the latter around. I gave an illogical answer to how many people it takes to screw in a light bulb. Why did the chicken cross the road? The chicken wanted to get to the other side of the road. That was a logical answer, but what makes it illogical is that you're supposed to give an illogical answer. Any illogical answer could in some instances be considered a joke.

Proposition: An inmate is eligible for parole. For the last two years the inmate has been in a prison gang exploiting other inmates. Premise: You're now eligible for parole why should we parole you? Induction: I've done more than half my time. Premise: What achievements have you made since you've been here? Induction: I've gotten my GED. Deduction: I think you should give me my parole because now that I have a GED I can get a good job and stay out of prison. Premise: We have reports of you belonging to a prison gang who exploits other prisoners. Deduction: I had no choice but to join or they would've killed me. I didn't want to join the gang and I don't believe in what they stand for and I would like to get paroled so I can get away from them. Illogical predicate of the proposition: Your parole is granted. We wish you good luck.

The parole board that is our last line of defense against a criminal getting out of prison and back into our society failed to make a logical conclusion. Now the prison gang member is a street gang member and can get his hands on machine guns, grenade launchers, and heat seeking missiles not to mention all the drugs he could sell. He'll be able to mail in money to the fellow gang members who are still in prison, in which they can use the money to get into more powerful position to exploit even more people. It was a joke for the parole board to allow the inmate gang member to be realest on parole, now the only thing is nobody's laughing.

When people come to an illogical answer there are only two possible reasons. Reason one: They failed to see all of the premises. Reason two: They didn't believe all the premises to be true. Things we believe to be true we consider to-be our knowledge. So to the best of his or her knowledge the parole board did the right thing by paroling the inmate. They either missed the premise, that gang member are gang members for life or they believed the inmate was telling the true in saying, "I don't believe in what they stand for and want to be paroled so I can get away from them." In this complicated world the inmate could in fact be telling the truth as well. The world is a very complicated place in deed.

We base what we believe to be true, which is our knowledge, on our preexisting knowledge of the world. Things that are perceived as knowledge can in fact be universal knowledge that we've adopted from other people. Proposition: If I can find a rock that floats in mid-air I could sell it for twice the price of the hope diamond. Premise: It's a universal knowledge that there is no rock on the earth that floats in mid-air instead of falling to the ground. Deduction: Did you go around the world and pick up each and every single rock and check to make sure they all fall and none floats in mid-air? Premise: It would take more than a lifetime to go around the world and check if each and every rock falls when you drop it. Induction: People have lived on the earth for thousands of years and nobody ever found a rock that floats in mid-air instead of falling to the ground when you drop it. Induction: It's a universal knowledge that's never been proved wrong. Predicate of the proposition: There is no rock on this earth that floats in mid-air instead of falling to the ground when you drop it. Therefore it's okay to base our logical conclusions on universal knowledge of what we believe to be true because it would in fact take more than a lifetime to check every rock in the world.

Let's see what happens if somebody doesn't believe all of the premises. Proposition: I can sell drugs without getting caught and going to prison. Premise: All drug dealers go to prison because all drug dealers get caught dealing the drugs out on the streets. Deduction: I'll only sell to people I know. Premise: You have to sell a lot of drugs to make a living at it. Deduction: I'll sell in massive quantities to people I know. Premise: If the police catch them with the drug they'll turn you over to get a lesser sentence. Deduction: My people wouldn't do that to me. Premise: You're responsible for your mind and your actions only and can't assume what his or her actions will be. Induction: People on drugs have no code of ethics and are only interested in him or her selves. Induction: All roads lead back to the dealer. Deduction: I only deal with stand up people and they would never do that to me. Premise: What if one of your stand up people gives some drugs to one of his or her friends who you don't know and they get caught and turn your friends in? Deduction: Like I said, "My people would take the fall without turning me in as well." Illogical predicate of the proposition: He can sell drugs without getting caught by the police. The drug dealer didn't believe the premises to be true so he's basing his logic on what he believes to be true, which isn't true. His illogical answer will someday come crashing in on him.

Failure to see all possible premises or not believing all the premises to be true will get you an illogical answer every time. Illogical answers are nothing more than punch lines that are used in-jokes. One way to avoid getting an illogical answer is to do your logical premises and propositions with another person, friend, or lover. If there is two people working on one premise or logical problem then it's less likely that both of you will miss all the premises. If you don't believe a premise to be true you might want to ask yourself why you don't believe it to be true. Some times after reconsidering a premise it'll start to make sense to you.

Once you get the basics down you can apply logic to anything you want a logical answer on. Proposition: If a tree falls in the woods and nobody is there to hear it, does it still make a noise? Premise: If you were there to hear it, would it make a noise? Deduction: If you're not there to hear it then how do you truly know it makes a noise? Premise: The external world exists even when, we're not perceiving it. Induction: If the world exists even though we cannot perceive it, then yes, it would make a noise. Predicate of the proposition: Yes, it makes a noise even if nobody heard it. What do you know it works?

I want to improve my life but I don't know what I want. Proposition: How can I improve my life if I have no idea what I want? Premise: What are some of the things you like to do? Induction: I like working with children. Premise: Maybe you should look into a career with children. Deduction: I don't have any skills working with children. Premise: Maybe you could go to school and learn. Deduction: I don't have money to pay for school. Premise: There are grants and student loans that'll pay for the tuition today that you can pay back later. Deduction: I don't have the time to go to school. Premise: If you keep making excuses you'll be condemned to live life the way you're living it now. Predicate of the proposition: There are always excuses not to improve your life but if there's a will there's a way. Change usually happens when things get so unbearable that change is unavoidable.

This concludes this chapter on business logic. Logic is to philosophy and small business management what mathematics is to science. Please try and practice these basic logical skills and if you master them and I think you can, you'll never be as confused as before you started studying logic. Logic can be used to answer questions you want answered in a more affirmative way. Logically correct answers need very little explanations if any. Use logic to make your business plans to open your own small business. Use logic wisely, boldly, but never sparingly. Now go get your goals!

Afterword

Further reading

"The Darkness Below": ISBN#-0877146934, by Lee A. Eide. The author's writing has appeared in "Referee Magazine" a nationally distributed publication targeted toward sports officials, and the "Upper Room" a worldwide daily devotional guide for Christians. Mr. Eide has completed three writing courses from "Writer's Digest Writing Schools", including one on novel writing. In the Darkness Below, Victoria Mayfield's lucid dreams of a Messianic figure on a mystical journey in another world and the formation of an international, bloodthirsty cult in our world can both be traced back to Halloween party from Victoria's childhood. From the back street canals of Venice to the heights of, "Ulangstias' mountain-castle in Grandeur to the depths of the human heart, the novel takes the reader on a powerful literary journey of a lifetime. A must read book by Lee A. Eide. Also available now on E-Book or hardcopy.

To order the "Darkness Below" go to the publisher's web site at: *www.thebookden.com* and search for the author's name or book title or go directly to the book site at: *www.galaxymall.com/retail/destiny/darkness.html*. The book will be available by December 2000.

"Dead Man's Plan" ISBN#-0877145687, also by Lee A. Eide. Greed, a Hollywood actor's galaxy-sized ego, and corporate welfare threaten to destroy a small town in South Dakota. A transplanted ex-accountant and the collective spirit of the old west form a bizarre alliance that may save the town but can the stories hero, Lee Wyatt, survive the electric chair?

Conclusions

What is Philosophy? Philosophy is derived from the Greek word meaning love of wisdom. Philosophy is a way of thinking about certain sorts of questions. Philosophy's most distinctive feature is its use of logical arguments to evaluate the problems that was put to the philosopher. If an American says, "This is my philosophy." what they're really saying, "This is my personal outlook on that." Philosophers basically deal in arguments. They'll criticize other people's views or invent new views. They also analyze and clarify concepts. Most Americans use the word philosophy like it's their statement of what they believe. Philosophy is practiced, by working in a tradition of arguing myths and other points of beliefs. Usually on topics most Americans take for granted. Questions like what is reality? What is the meaning of life? Is there a God? What is memory? Philosophers question the unquestionable things most people take for granted. By doing so they get a better understanding of the external world around them and some times having a better understanding can in a way give inner peace to the philosopher.

If a small business manager uses philosophy to decide how to run a small business, it's my opinion that he or she will do a better job and be more successful. Small business entrepreneurs can also benefit from using philosophy to start their own business. Understanding these simple philosophies can give individuals open-mindedness, which is always beneficial in small business, especially today. The more you know, the farther you go. Regards Francis A. Olivo.

About the Author

I possibly should have named the book, "How to Think Like a Hippie Philosopher." I spent my share of life, foot lose and fancy free. When I was 19 years old I moved to New York City and lived out of an old van all summer trying to make it in the big apple. I was a truck driver for years traveling all over the USA and I've been to all of the states at least once. I skydived in 1994, but only did one free-fall jump. I've learned to fly small airplanes but I was VFR only I never went into instrument ratings. I canoed down the Colorado River in 1989, and went fly-fishing in Montana. I went on a cross-country motorcycle trip for three months with two friends and camped out alone side highways or near by forests. I drank a lot of wine & cognac and listened to a lot of songs and met a lot of America's finest women. At times in my life I've had hair half way down my back, I've got more tattoos than some philately collectors have stamps. I've had more high society people stick their nose up at me than anybody else I can think of. One thing is for sure; I know what having or owning a life means to me. I have no regrets about any of these things. My friends kept telling me Frank you've gotta write a book on philosophy. So I wanted to write something that could help my fellow Americans rather than just write something of purely entertainment value only. That's why I wrote the Olivononics and Olivofonics series of books.

So allow me to tell you my philosophies on what I believe to be real. I believe that a sperm cell has a mind of its own because how does it know to swim to the egg? I believe the egg has a mind of its own but for some reason isn't able to move under its own power. When the sperm and egg unite they form one human being, yet the minds don't splice together. If the egg splits in two and forms twins I think the sperm's mind and the egg's mind also splits evenly into two pieces as well so each twin has both a conscious and subconscious mind.

I believe the sperm's mind becomes our conscious mind because our conscious mind seems to be in charge of making the decisions on how to move our bodies. Since it's the sperm cell that swims over to the egg than it must have a mind or at the very least instinct of how to get to the egg. I believe that it's the egg's mind that becomes our subconscious mind because the egg doesn't have any control on how to move but must have a mind or at the very least instinct to keep its heart and other such organs working.

So if a mind can split into two evenly but can't splice together than it's possible that our mind could be split off from our parents mind. Our parents mind could also be split off from their parents mind as well and so on and so on until we get to the first mind in existence. How did the first mind come into existence? Maybe something beautiful happened thousands of years ago that created the human mind and we simply don't know what that something might in fact be. Just because we don't understand something doesn't mean it can't be so. Did God create the human mind? I believe that even though our minds are split off the original mind, when we die we no longer exist and go back into the same existence we were in before we were born. Again, just because you can't understand something doesn't mean it's not true.

So I'm an agnostic person who can't truly call myself an atheist because my conclusions are not based on logical predicate of the propositions. I'm an atheist out of blind faith that my philosophies are in fact true. The premise: I don't know where the original mind came from, is one that I can't answer so therefore I'm basing my conclusion on blind faith rather than on logic. Until I can deduct all possible premises I'm stuck with blind faith to base my conclusion on. We live in a truly complicated world. Answers to some questions have to be based on blind faith. That's the same way that Christian bases their beliefs as well.

There is no rock that floats in mid-air instead of falling to the ground when you drop it. This is a universal knowledge and shouldn't come as a surprise to you. How do we know this to be true? Did anybody go around the world and pick up each and every single rock and drop it to make sure it fell to the ground and didn't float in mid-air? If somebody did in fact go around the world checking each rock and did find one that floated in mid-air would that person tell others about it. A rock that floats in mid-air would be worth more than the hope diamond. Why should this person tell anybody they have a priceless rock? Do we base the knowledge of there's no rock that floats in mid-air on blind faith and assume it to be universal knowledge that there's no rock that floats in mid-air? That's a universal knowledge, wouldn't you agree? People have never found a rock that floats in mid-air. Therefore there isn't one.

In order to think like a philosopher you must not miss any of the premises. If you think that there's no rock that floats in mid-air than you've missed a premise. I know for sure that there is one rock that floats in mid-air. It does in fact truly exist. It's worth more than the hope diamond, yet people don't give it a second though to its value. The rock is right under your nose or should I say feet. The name of the rock that floats in mid-air is called, "Earth." Therefore even universal knowledge can also be wrong. Yet, mankind is to eager to draw conclusions that it misses to many premises and comes up with illogical answers as well. In our eagerness do we pass bad or wrongful judgements? In order for a person to come up with a logical answer there can be no premises that can't be explained. Until the time we have all the logical answers it's our duty to recognize the fact that we can be wrong in our logic and in our judgements. Even though the urge to base our decisions on blind faith, is at times, overwhelming we must acknowledge the fact that humans are imperfect and don't have all the answers.

Is it no more than blind faith that give the person the idea that they should buy a supper sonic car with payments they can hardly afford? Is it blind faith that makes rich people snub his or her noses at people performing hard labor jobs rather than high society jobs? I've had all kinds of manual labor jobs and some people viewed me as, "A nobody." Is it blind faith that makes people believe what they do? Things you believe you consider being your knowledge. If you don't believe something then you have no knowledge of that thing.

As long as people push aside his or her preexisting knowledge to create make-believe realities, how can mankind expect to progress any farther? People, who push aside their preexisting knowledge because to do the right thing is such a hassle and it's much easier to make a new reality than to go through and do all the correct stuff, are only fooling him or her self. Some people's idea of helping mankind is to get a lot of awards to hang on the wall and point to it and say, "Look what I did for my contribution to mankind." Is a college graduate a guarantee of a better person, than one who dropped out of school?

I believe that people change when his or her present situation gets so unbearable that change is unavoidable. People get to this stage because they push aside their preexisting knowledge and make up false realities to get out of doing the right thing in the first place. Then the real reality comes crashing into his or hers false sense of reality and they're miserable once again and still make up a new reality to deal with it. What is so hard about thinking that we would rather make up lies to ourselves and live in a false reality? People will commit suicide rather than do some thing, which they know is what they should've done in the first place. Why does it always have to get to the point of being unbearable before anybody wants to change? People who live in a false reality are condemned to live the bad experience over and over again.

People mindlessly going through life without ever asking, "What do I value about my life?" or "What do I consider having or owning a life to be?" Everybody has his or her own version of what having or owning a life is. Yet people change their minds about what they want and don't want faster than the wind changes directions. Is life to see who can make the most money in the shortest amount of time? Life is too short to waste it trying to collect a lot of worldly possessions. Until you can take a stand on what having or owning a life is to you, then you're going to be confused of what you want. Confusion living in America is due to the illusion that it's important to get a lot of stuff in order to be successful. With all the relentless ads on supper deluxe this and that it's easy to get confused on where to make a stand.

Well that concludes Olivofonics: Small Business Management & Philosophy for Beginners. This book was designed to get you to think in a more philosophical manner, while considering opening your own small business. I basically covered the philosophies and topics to get you to think like a philosopher and have some kind of an idea of what goes into opening your own business. Anybody in my same situation would've done the same thing so that makes my maxim, "Write enough to get him or her thinking like a philosopher and future entrepreneurs, plus keep the book short and sweet." Morally correct in Kant's philosophy of ethics. Let's test your philosophical powers. I've enclosed a poem that I wrote last year. It is your duty to pick out all the philosophical premises in the poem. Good luck and I give you my utmost highest respect and best wishes. Regards Frank...

Laureato

Graduation was soon to come.
Nobody knew what would be done.
The classes started when the bell had rung.
The school was old, and the children young.
Guns were pulled and the shooting had begun.
They ran far and wide but many had died.
I wasn't sure if my eyes had lied.
Two classmate killers: laughing with pride.
Shooting the ones that did not hide.
Blood flowed everywhere just like the tide.
Standing so close there was no time to bide.
I ran hard and grabbed his side.
He pulled his trigger and got my eye.
I fell over but did not die.
I looked at him and asked him, "why?"
"Cause you're a jock" was his only reply.
I lied on the floor in such great pain.
As the classmate killers made their fame.
It doesn't matter who's to blame.
Any reason would be so lame.
To kill so many: over an old flame.
They shoot and kill and have no shame.
Both of them were insane.
The police arrived but in their vain.
Were eight dead bodies just the same.
I didn't die today you see.
For some strange reason they let me be.
Now I lecture to you for free.
To try and stop the shooting spree.

Prejudice is not my cup of tea.
It's the devil's work and you let it be.
We all have a right to be.
Especially: in the land of the free.
Love and peace is the way to be.
Living together in harmony.
Whether it's ebony or ivory.
I say always get along, naturally.

Appendix

Employee Labor Laws

Fair Labor Standards Act

In the processing of payrolls, the first step is to determine gross pay. The fair labor standards act "FLSA" of 1938 affects this calculation. Commonly referred to as the federal wage and hour law, this law sets up minimum wage, currently $5.15 per hour, and overtime pays requirements. Other provisions of this law concern equal pay for equal work regardless of sex, restrictions upon the employment of child labor, public service contracts, and wage garnishment. These basic provisions apply to employers engaged in interstate commerce and to employees in certain enterprises, which are so engaged, unless specifically exempted. The "FLSA" also imposes record keeping requirements on employers, however, prescribes no specific form of record.

State Minimum Wage and Maximum Hours Law.

Most states have established minimum wage rates for covered employees, either by legislation or by administration order of the legislature whereby minimum wage rates are fixed for specific industries. As I wrote earlier, the fair labor standards act, a federal law, also applies minimum wage and maximum hours provisions to employers. Where both federal and state regulations cover the same employee, the higher of the two rates prevails. In Alaska, for example, the minimum hourly wage is $5.65, or $0.50 more than the federal minimum wage requirements.

Civil Rights Act of 1964.

Title 7 of the civil rights act of 1964, entitled, "Equal Employment Opportunity," provides for several fair employment practices. The act, as amended, forbids employers to discriminate in hiring, firing, promoting, compensating, or in any other condition of employment on the basis of race, color, religion, sex, or national origin. Guidelines, established by the "Equal Employment Opportunity Commission" or "EEOC", also include physical characteristics in the definition of national origin discrimination. The "EEOC" has also established and declared that sexual harassment violates the civil rights act. Unwelcome sexual advances, request for sexual favors, and other verbal and or physical conduct of a sexual nature can constitute sexual harassment. The "EEOC" prohibits unions and employment agencies from including or segregating their members on the basis of race, color, religion, sex, or national origin.

Executive Order 11246

This is the major nondiscrimination regulation for government contractors and subcontractors who perform work under federal construction contract that exceed $10,000.00 and for the United States government itself. Covered contractors must scrutinize tests and other screening procedures and make all changes necessary to assure nondiscrimination. They must also post notices announcing their nondiscrimination responsibilities in the place conspicuous to employees, applicants, and representatives of each labor union with which the contractors deal.

Age Discrimination in Employment Act or "ADEA"

The age discrimination in employment act of 1967 prohibits employers, employment agencies, and labor unions from discriminating on the basis of age in their employment practices. The act covers only employers, who employ 20 or more employees, employment agencies, and labor unions engaged in an industry affecting interstate commerce. The act also covers federal, state, and local government employees, other than elected officials and certain aides not covered by civil service. The "ADEA" provides protection for almost all employees over the age of 40. A key exception involves executives who are 65 or older and who've held high policymaking positions during the two-year period before retirement. If such an employee is entitled to an annual retirement benefit from the employer of at least $44,000.00, currently, the employee can be forcible retired. In order to provide proof of compliance with the various fair employment laws, employers must keep accurate personnel and payroll records. All employment applications, notices of being fired and reason of being fired, and employment history should be kept.

Americans with Disabilities Act "ADA"

The Americans with disabilities act of 1990 prohibits employers, with 15 or more employees, employment agencies, labor unions, and management committees from discriminating against qualified persons with disabilities because of their disability. The prohibition of disability-based discrimination applies to job application procedures, hiring, advancement, firing, compensation, job training, and any other conditions of employment. In addition, reasonable accommodations, such as ramp for wheelchairs, restrooms, and any other a commendations to help disability people get around including fire escapes.

Income Tax withholding laws

With the passage of the 16th Amendment in 1913, taxation of income became constitutional. Today, an income tax is levied on the earnings of most employees and is deducted from their gross pay. In some cases, this may involve three separate deductions from the employee's gross pay, a federal income tax, a state federal tax, and a local or city income tax or wage tax. All of the acts that levy these various income taxes provide for the collection of taxes at the source of the wages paid or payroll withholding. Most states impose state income taxes on individuals. The laws vary from state to state as to the amount to be held, exemptions from withholding, and the time for withholding reports to be filed. Employers may also be required by state income tax laws to deduct and withhold local income taxes on salaries or wages paid.

Federal Insurance Contributions Act or "FICA"

Better known as the social security program planned by the federal government to provide economic security for workers and their families. The act levies a tax on employers and employees in certain industries to be paid to the federal government and credited to the federal old-age, survivors, and disability insurance or "OASDI" tax levied on employees is a set percentage of their gross wages, and it must be withheld from their paychecks. From these funds, the federal government makes payments to persons who are entitled to the benefits under the social security act. FICA also provides a health insurance program, commonly known as "Medicare" for the aged and disabled.

Federal Unemployment Tax Act or "FUTA"

Like the federal insurance contribution act, FUTA is incorporated in the internal revenue code. If an employer employs one or more individuals in each of 20 or more weeks in occupations covered by FUTA or pays wages of $1,500.00 or more during any calendar year, a federal unemployment insurance tax must be paid. The federal government uses the collected tax to pay state and federal administrative expenses of the unemployment program. Employers subjected to FUTA receive credit against most of the FUTA tax when they contribute to their state unemployment compensation fund usually called, "SUTA"

State Unemployment Tax Act or "SUTA"

All fifty states and the District of Columbia have enacted unemployment insurance laws. Each employer receives a credit against FUTA tax because of the contribution to the state's unemployment program. The taxes paid to the individual state by employers are used primarily for the payment of unemployment benefits. The social security act specifies certain standards that each state has to meet in passing an unemployment compensation law. These standards have resulted in fairly high degree of uniformity in the requirements of state unemployment laws and in records that must be kept by the businesses. State laws do differ, however, making it necessary for employers to be familiar with the laws of the state in which they do business. The unemployment compensation laws require employers to keep payroll records similar to those required under the federal law. Large penalties may be imposed for failure to keep the required records, for failure or delinquency in making the required returns, or for default or delinquency in paying the contributions. The required period for retaining records varies in different states, but in no case should the records be kept for a period of less than four years because of the federal requirement. Personally I would keep them for five years.

Paying Less then minimum wage, under certain conditions, wages lower than the minimum wage may be paid to some employees. Retail or service establishments and farms may employ full-time students at 85% of the minimum wage, which currently would be $4.38 per hour. Institutions of higher education may employ their own full-time students at 85% of the minimum wage. Student-learners may be employed at 75% of the minimum wage if they are participating in a bona fide vocational training program conducted by an accredited school, currently $3.86 per hour. Persons whose earning capacity is impaired by age, physical or mental deficiency, or injury may be employed at special minimum wage rates. However, a certificate authorizing employment at such rates must first be issued. This is a great way to save money and help your fellow man. Never assume anything about laws on minimum wage always check with the Department of Employment in your state or county before going below the federal minimum wage guidelines.

Glossary

Adequate: Equal to what is required or fully sufficient on how to act in certain situations.

Aristotle (384 BC-322BC): Ancient Greek philosopher and student to Plato.

Atheist: Somebody who doesn't believe that God or Gods exists.

Blaise Pascal: (1623-1662) Famous for the Pascal's Wager philosophy.

Brain: Organ in the human body believed to be where the mind exists.

Causal Realism: The way you can make your way around the external world by using preexisting knowledge along with your senses.

Claustrophobia: Fear of being in very small rooms.

Common Realism: The way people who have never studied philosophy make their way around in the external world.

Communism: A society based on the state owning the means in which people make their living on.

Conquentialism: A philosophy on ethics that looks at the out come of an action along with the person's intentions of why they did the action.

Consequentialist: Somebody who believes in the consequentialism philosophy.

Deontological: Another name for duty based philosophies.

Dualism: Somebody who believes the mind is separate from the body and can go on after death into an after life.

Elitism: Viewed that formation of elites in some sphere is desirable, and that the status and privileges of existing elites are worth protecting.

Etiquette: Norms of a polite society.

Euthanasia: Best known as mercy killing. Comes in two forms, passive and active euthanasia.

Exploitation: Crime of taking advantage of people for your benefit and not theirs.

Francis A. Olivo: (1963-?) Philosopher and poet and writer trying to help people live up to their fullest potential.

Friedrich Engels: (1820-1895) Helped write the Communist Manifesto in 1848.

George Berkeley: (1685-1753) Famous Idealism philosophy philosopher.

Hallucinations: Illusions that people consider to be real.

Immanuel Kant (1724-1804) Famous philosopher known for his duty based philosophy on ethics.

Insanity: Somebody who's not in touch with the real world or does the same thing over and over again and expects a different result.

Instincts: Non-taught biological capabilities.

Jean Piaget: (1896-1980) Swiss psychologist most famous for his research on the development of reasoning in children.

John Stuart Mill: (1806-1873) famous for his Utilitarianism philosophy on ethics.

Karl Marx: (1818-1883) Wrote the Communist Manifesto in 1848 to exploit working people.

Masochist: Somebody who finds pleasure in inflicting pain or receiving pain.

Maxim: The intentions behind somebody doing an act.

Mind: A possibly Non-physical or physical entity that exists in the brain or so we believe.

Metaphysics: Relates to any inquires that science is unable to track down an answer to. Deals mostly with the philosophical theory of reality. Was originally a title from Aristotle's physics.

Olivononics: (Oh-Lee-Vo-Non-Eks) A system of self-help developed by Francis A. Olivo.

Ontological: A branch of meta-physics dealing with the philosophical theory of reality.

Paranoia: Excessive worrying about make-believe dangers.

Physicalism: Believes that the mind and body are one and the same and that there is no life after death.

Physicalist: Somebody who believes in physicalism.

Plato: (428-348 BC) Ancient Greek philosopher and teacher to Aristotle.

Rene Descartes: (1596-1650) Famous philosopher who said, "I think therefore I am." Dualist by heart.

Samaritan: Know as Good Samaritan help people in need.

Suicide: Somebody taking their own life.

Syllogism: A philosophy in logic developed by Aristotle where the conclusion is based on the predicate of two premises or propositions. This was used up till the 1900's.

Universal Knowledge: Is based on what is commonly known about the external world by lots of people.

Utilitarianism: Also know as the greatest happiness philosophy of ethics.

www.ingramcontent.com/pod-product-compliance
Lightning Source LLC
Chambersburg PA
CBHW031052180526
45163CB00002BA/793